THE ORDNANCE SURVEY
JOURNEY THROUGH TIME

Can **YOU** solve over 300
puzzles on an adventure
through history and landscape?

Ordnance
Survey

By Ordnance Survey and Tim Dedopulos

Mapping images © Crown Copyright and database rights 2021
Text and other images © Ordnance Survey Limited 2021
Puzzles © The Orion Publishing Group Ltd 2021
Puzzles by Tim Dedopulos

The right of the Ordnance Survey to be identified as
the authors of this work has been asserted in accordance with the
Copyright, Designs and Patents Act 1988.

This edition first published in Great Britain in 2021 by
Trapeze
an imprint of the Orion Publishing Group Ltd
Carmelite House
50 Victoria Embankment
London EC4Y 0DZ

An Hachette UK Company

13 5 7 9 10 8 6 4 2

ISBN: 978 1 3987 0706 1

Printed in Italy

The names OS and Ordnance Survey and the OS logos are protected by UK trade
mark registrations and/or are trademarks of Ordnance Survey Limited, Great Britain's
national mapping agency.

Every effort has been made to fulfil requirements with regard to
reproducing copyright material. The author and publisher will be
glad to rectify any omissions at the earliest opportunity.

www.orionbooks.co.uk

CONTENTS

▓ Introduction 6

▓ Common Map Abbreviations and Symbols . . . 8

▓ An Introduction to the Puzzles 10

▓ A New Adventure. 11

PUZZLES

■ Prehistoric, Mesolithic and Neolithic 15

■ Romans 29

■ Medieval 49

■ Tudors 77

■ Stuarts 95

▓ Georgians 105

■ Victorians 127

■ Twentieth Century 157

▓ Solutions. 191

▓ Ordnance Survey Map Information 234

▓ Credits 238

▓ Acknowledgements 239

INTRODUCTION

Great Britain is steeped in history. Events from prehistoric ages through to today have shaped our entire landscape. The outcome of the actions of our forefathers are evident in many of our maps, from Neolithic stone monuments to Roman forts, once inhabited caves to disused railways, castles to churches. The list is endless. So much has changed due to human actions, some for the better, some not so applaudable. While our very recently written history, with the restrictions and life changing events that have come with it, may be something we wish to forget, for the time being at least, looking further back through time is fascinating. If only we had a time machine.

At Ordnance Survey we are proud of our history but also of our reputation as leaders in geospatial technology. Our innovative approach isn't something exclusive to the modern day; back in 1747 it was the innovative young engineer William Roy who created a military map of Scotland aged just twenty-one, with no military experience, and then voiced a bigger ambition, to survey and map the whole of Britain. In 1791 the British government, concerned by turmoil in Europe and the French Revolution, ordered its defensive ministry – The Board of Ordnance – to begin surveying England's vulnerable southern coasts. Tasked with producing the most precise mapping possible to guide the military around our island, Ordnance Survey was born.

We've long since moved on from the days of painstakingly measuring land features and drawing maps by hand, although many of our triangulation pillars still stand today and provide a worthy tribute to the early cartographers. Technological advances have allowed us to collect data more rapidly and accurately. The way that data is used is changing, our digital services are under more demand than ever before, and our teams are constantly seeking new and better ways to deliver the data that can help our customers solve their problems or to plan their next adventure.

Today you can access our maps in many ways: on paper, online and though our apps. All are designed to help you get outside more often, to help you plan your adventures and see more of the wonderful landscape around you – and we hope that, on completing these puzzles, you'll be inspired to start an adventure, seek out the history of your local area and create your own memories in the great outdoors.

We'd love to hear from you on our social media pages, using the tag #OSPuzzleTime. Find us on Twitter @OSleisure, Instagram @ordnancesurvey and Facebook @osmapping.

Nick Giles

Managing Director – Ordnance Survey Leisure

COMMON MAP ABBREVIATIONS AND SYMBOLS

SELECTED TOURIST AND LEISURE SYMBOLS

🏛	Art gallery (notable / important)	Ⓜ	Museum
	Boat hire		National Trust
	Boat trips		Nature reserve
	Building of historic interest	☆	Other tourist feature
	Cadw (Welsh Heritage)	P	Parking
Å	Camp site	P&R	Park and ride, all year
	Camping and caravan site	P&R	Park and ride, seasonal
	Caravan site	ℂ ℂ	Phone; public, emergency
	Castle or fort	⊠	Picnic site
✝	Cathedral or abbey		Preserved railway
	Country park		Public house(s)
	Craft centre		Public toilets
	Cycle hire	Ⓧ	Recreation, leisure or sports centre
	Cycle trail		Slipway
	English Heritage		Theme or pleasure park
	Fishing		Viewpoint
	Garden or arboretum	V	Visitor centre
	Golf course or links	!	Walks or trails
HC	Heritage centre		Water activities (board)
	Historic Scotland		Water activities (paddle)
U	Horse riding		Water activities (powered)
i	Information centre		Water activities (sailing)
i	Information centre, seasonal		Watersports centre (multi-activity)
	Mountain bike trail	◎	World Heritage site / area

ABBREVIATIONS

Acad	Academy	Ind Est	Industrial Estate	Rd	Road
BP	Boundary Post	La	Lane	Rems	Remains
BS	Boundary Stone	LC	Level Crossing	Resr	Reservoir
CG	Cattle Grid	Liby	Library	Rly	Railway
CH	Clubhouse	Mkt	Market	Sch	School
Cotts	Cottages	Meml	Memorial	St	Saint / Street
Dis	Disused	MP	Milepost	Twr	Tower
Dismtd	Dismantled	MS	Milestone	TH	Town Hall
Fm	Farm	Mon	Monument	Uni	University
F Sta	Fire Station	PH	Public House	NTL	Normal Tidal Limit
FB	Footbridge	P, PO	Post Office	Wks	Works
Ho	House	Pol Sta	Police station	°W; Spr	Well; Spring

PUBLIC RIGHTS OF WAY

- - - - - - - - - - - Footpath

— — — — — Bridleway

-+- -+- -+- -+- -+- Byway open to all traffic

-+- -+- -+- -+- -+- Restricted byway (no vehicles)

The symbols show the defined route so far as the scale of mapping will allow. Rights of way are liable to change and may not be clearly defined on the ground. Rights of way are not shown on maps of Scotland, where rights of responsible access apply.

PUBLIC ACCESS

● ● ● Other public routes (not normally shown in urban areas)

◆ ◆ ◆ Way-marked recreational route

National Trail

Scotland's Great Trails

The representation on the maps of any other road, track or path is no evidence of the existence of a right of way.

ACCESS LAND (England and Wales)

Access land

Access land in wooded area

within sand

Coastal margin

Access land portrayed on this map is intended as a guide to land normally available for access on foot, for example access land created under the Countryside and Rights of Way Act 2000, and land managed by National Trust, Forestry England, Woodland Trust and Natural Resources Wales. Some restrictions will apply; some land shown as access land may not have open access rights; always refer to local signage.

The depiction of rights of access does not imply or express any warranty as to its accuracy or completeness. Observe local signs and follow the Countryside Code. Visit: **gov.uk/government/publications/the-countryside-code**

OTHER ACCESS (Scotland)

National Trust for Scotland, always open

National Trust for Scotland, limited access – observe local signs

Forestry and Land Scotland, normally open – observe local signs

Woodland Trust Land

All land within the 'coastal margin' (where it already exists) is associated with the England Coast Path (**nationaltrail.co.uk/england-coast-path**) and is by default access land, but in some areas it contains land not subject to access rights and land subject to local restrictions including many areas of saltmarsh and flats that are not suitable for public access. The coastal margin is often steep, unstable and not readily accessible. Please take careful note of conditions and local signage on the ground.

In Scotland, everyone has access rights in law* over most land and inland water, provided access is exercised responsibly. The **Scottish Outdoor Access Code** is the reference point for responsible behaviour, and can be obtained at **outdooraccess-scotland.com**.

HEIGHTS AND NATURAL FEATURES

Water

Mud

Sand

Contours   Vertical face/cliff

Loose rock   Boulders   Outcrop   Scree

Survey height;

52 ·   Ground

284 ·   Air

Surface heights are to the nearest metre above mean sea level.

LAND FEATURES

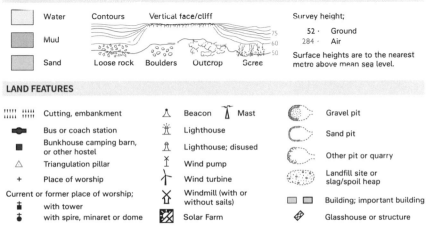

!!!!! !!!!!
!!!!! !!!!! Cutting, embankment

Bus or coach station

Bunkhouse camping barn, or other hostel

△ Triangulation pillar

+ Place of worship

Current or former place of worship;

with tower

with spire, minaret or dome

⅄ Beacon   Ⱦ Mast

Lighthouse

Lighthouse; disused

Wind pump

Wind turbine

Windmill (with or without sails)

Solar Farm

Gravel pit

Sand pit

Other pit or quarry

Landfill site or slag/spoil heap

Building; important building

Glasshouse or structure

AN INTRODUCTION TO PUZZLES

You are about to set off on a puzzle adventure through the greatest moments in British history. It's a journey through time that will leave you astounded, as you travel alongside the formidable Aunt Bea, whose knowledge knows no bounds. No undertaking of this sort could ever be definitive and there were stops that could not be made and will have to wait for next time. We hope that, like Aunt Bea, you will be inspired to explore the rich treasures to be found all around us.

The puzzles she has uncovered contain something for everyone: a mix of word puzzles, search-and-find clues and general knowledge questions, as well as navigation conundrums to satisfy the more skilled map-readers.* Pay careful attention to Aunt Bea in the sections before the puzzles too, as she's been known to give away clues. You may sometimes even have to find answers to questions that can't be solved with the map, so keep your wits about you.

Questions are split into four levels of difficulty:

■ **Easy**

■ **Medium**

■ **Tricky**

■ **Challenging**

We hope you finish this adventure celebrating the hidden treasures to be found throughout time and that these maps, stories and puzzles encourage you to think again about your place in history, your local area, and perhaps take a look at a map and imagine, as Aunt Bea does, those that have walked upon it and in whose footprints you can follow.

* For those of you that aren't map whizzes just yet, remember the following: ground survey heights are marked on the maps in black, air survey heights are marked in orange, and the vertical interval between contour lines is usually 5 metres but in mountainous regions it may well be 10 metres, so be careful!

A new adventure

'Every journey on a map, my boy, is a journey through time as well as space.'

My Aunt Bea is always saying things like this. We were trudging up over a hill, low clouds on the horizon threatening rain. As ever, she was way out in front of me, gesticulating wildly, as I puffed along in the distance behind her.

'Here the straight edge of a Roman road, there a place name bequeathed to us by the Saxons, or maybe the Vikings, the Normans and everyone who's been here before and since. And beneath it all the bones of deep time, older than humans can imagine, a land that remembers long before we arrived and I am sure will endure long after we have gone.'

She reached the brow of the hill and stopped, stretching her arm out in front of her signalling the view spread out before us.

'But maps are only ever one part of a journey. To truly appreciate how it all fits together, you have to get outside and feel it, to knit together time and space.'

We were on one of our sporadic adventures, in an ongoing attempt, in my aunt's words, to 'get me living in three dimensions and away from all those blasted screens'. (The fact that screens were really quite useful where maps were concerned didn't seem to have quite registered with her yet.)

Aunt Bea has always been obsessed with seeing as much of the country as possible. She claims our ancestor was part of the original Survey of Scotland mapping party with William Roy in 1747, the one that the Ordnance Survey originated with and that meant we were duty-bound to see as much of these islands as was possible.

What this meant in reality was that without warning, she'd arrive with her battered leather bag and books full of maps and clues and come and whisk me away for long walks, lectures on the hidden treasures of Britain and a variety of slightly dry home-made sandwiches.

It had all begun the week before with a letter

My dearest nephew,

The long summer break stretches out ahead of us imminently and I am determined that your brain is not to atrophy with your various pads and phones and computer gaming machines.

I have identified a new adventure for us. As ever, you will need good boots, waterproof clothes and a brain ready to solve the most cunning of clues. We are to take a trip of hundreds of thousands of years, so look sharp.

Yours excitedly,

Aunt Bea

Aunt Bea

As the train pulled into the station, she spotted me waiting at the door and waved frantically. As soon as I got off the train, she enveloped me in a massive hug that smelt as always of the mentholated cough sweets she constantly sucked.

'Let me look at you,' she said. 'You have grown, by my estimation, at least two feet since I last saw you.'

I checked around us to see if anyone was watching.

'Tell me, how is your historical knowledge, my boy?'

I must have given away the answer with my expression, because she smiled and narrowed her eyes.

'No matter. We are but two enthusiastic amateurs. What I want to show you is that history isn't just contained in castles and the great deeds of kings and queens, though of course we shall encounter a fair few of those on this strip. I want to show you how Britain is suffused with every different sort of history, and that with a little research, there is no place on these islands where we won't find a glimmering thread of history to pull upon.'

She suddenly swung a small bag into my hands.

'In here is everything we need to interpret our remarkable journey. One could spend a lifetime travelling the country and still never hope to capture the entirety of British history, of course. There's just too much of the stuff. So think of this as a very partial and personal route. There will be leaps and digressions, you can be sure of that. Unpicking the past is the journey of a lifetime. In that bag are the maps and clues we need to pick our particular route through thousands of years of history. A map is a kind of time machine, my boy. And it's time you learnt how to use it.'

Prehistoric, Mesolithic and Neolithic

Map 1 HAPPISBURGH

'It is hard to comprehend a million years, my boy, but that's pretty much how old they think the footprints they found down there were.'

We were standing, gazing out over a low cliff on to a pretty but unassuming sandy beach facing the North Sea. Along from us was a red-and-white-striped lighthouse like a barber's pole. In the distance a dog chased a ball in and out of the water.

'There was a storm in the spring of 2013, which uncovered these strange hollows preserved on the beach and they worked out that they were footprints. Analysing pollen in the sediment, they estimated they were between 850,000 and 950,000 years old.'

'That's nearly as old as you,' I said.

'That makes them the oldest evidence we have of humans in Britain. Homo antecessor. They used the measurements of the footprints and worked out the height and weight of whoever made them. Their best guess based on that is a group of children and adults. No evidence, but I like to think that it could have been a family.'

She gestured to a path down to the beach and we made our way down.

'It would have been far colder than it is now, more like winter in Scandinavia – a harsh life spent at the edges of pine forests with not a huge amount of edible plants. But there would have been horses, elks and mammoths.'

In the distance the dog looked up as if suddenly interested.

'Britain wasn't an island at that point. We were connected to what is now northern France by an enormous chalk ridge until it was washed away about 425,000 years ago. Those people were crossing the mudflats there and left their footprints. Over all those hundreds of thousands of years, as our various ancestors came and went, the land froze and thawed, emptied of human life and then more came from the continent – homo heidelbergensis, homo neanderthalensis and then homo sapiens.'

She nudged me. 'That's us. Such a huge expanse of time, so many lives, so much invisible to us. Long before language, there they were, living and dying. So many footprints gone forever, but we must always remember they were there at some point.'

We both stood as seabirds wheeled overhead.

'So much has changed, but the sea still tasted of salt, eh?'

Aunt Bea suddenly knelt down and for a moment I was worried, but then realised she was unlacing her boots.

'Now, I think it's only right to make some footprints of our own. And then, I rather think it's time to solve the first lot of our clues.'

■ Easy

1. What kind of tourist accommodation facilities are shown on the map?

2. How many farms have common colours in their name?

■ Medium

3. Which thoroughfare's name contains a word that is one letter change away from being an expression of disdain?

4. How many times does the word 'Farm' appear on the map?

■ Tricky

5. With respect to the map, which of the following is the odd one out: College, Manor, Grange, Lighthouse, Mill?

6. Which country is named on the map?

■ Challenging

7. Can you find locations on the map that are anagrams of the following words or phrases? Ignore the spaces and punctuation, which may differ from those in the place names.
    a. HEROES' FUN
    b. TARMAC OFFERS
    c. CRAG ADAPTOR
    d. BETTER RUGS

8. Starting at the lighthouse, head directly east to the coast. Follow the coastline to a telephone, and then take the road inland. Turn left at the crossroads. After passing another phone, turn right and follow the road to a tree. Head directly north from that tree to the second word which shares two letters with it. Find the most easterly instance of that word. Where are you?

Map 2 GOUGHS CAVE

'I just want to warn you, my boy. If at any point you make a joke about something I say being cheesy, I am leaving you here without a map.'

We were walking through a field with a steep cliff face to one side of us and some kind-faced but feral-looking sheep on the other.

'In a while we'll head down to the cave where they found Cheddar Man, the oldest, most complete skeleton we have in the British Isles. But before that I've always loved this countryside. Something about these hills and woods, the steep paths, earth and stone and wood. It feels like if you squint your eyes the modern world melts away and you could be standing 10,000 years ago.'

I turned around to look back down the path.

'Imagine we're in what's known as the Mesolithic, or Middle Stone Age. We've just come out of a period of intense cold when this island had reverted to glacial conditions. I want you to imagine parties of hunters loping through the woods, the sound of . . . you're thinking about the cheese sandwiches aren't you.'

I nodded sheepishly.

After we'd both had a round of cheese and pickle, we made our way back down the steep path tangled with tree roots, with Aunt Bea calling back over her shoulder.

'They found the skeleton in 1903 and at the time they estimated it to be around 90,000 years old, but in the seventies they carbon dated it and found it was more like 10,000 years old. Then in 2018, they were able to sequence the DNA from the skeleton and comparing it to contemporary records they recreated his face.'

We stood for a while to catch our breath.

'The data showed that he would most likely have had dark skin and pale eyes and dark brown hair. In the past it had often been thought that humans adapted with pale skin thousands of years earlier because pale skin is better at absorbing sunlight and producing vitamin D in low levels of sunlight. But our understanding of what those early Britons looked like has been transformed. His ancestors had likely come from the Middle East or Africa. This is an important reminder not to make assumptions about what the past looked like. So much of history was shaped by what a certain sort of man – one imagines with a moustache and a hat and possibly a pipe – thought was important. So much of the past has been like someone trying to see through a window but only seeing their own reflection. One of the most important things to keep in mind is how much more interesting Britain's history is than that.

Easy

1. Which named route is nearest to the highest air survey point on the map?

2. Which hole sounds like it is for the birds?

Medium

3. How many nature reserves are there, named or otherwise?

4. There are several locations named Combe or Coombe on the map. What is a combe?

Tricky

5. Which location shown on the map shares its name with a famous 1990 Tim Robbins movie?

6. Is the northerly angle formed by the intersection of Lyde Lane and Bradley Cross Lane greater or less than 65 degrees?

Challenging

7. The circle that has its centre at Pig's Hole and passes through the 174m ground survey height also passes through the names of which rocks?

8. Which ground survey heights shown on the map add up to a total of 578?

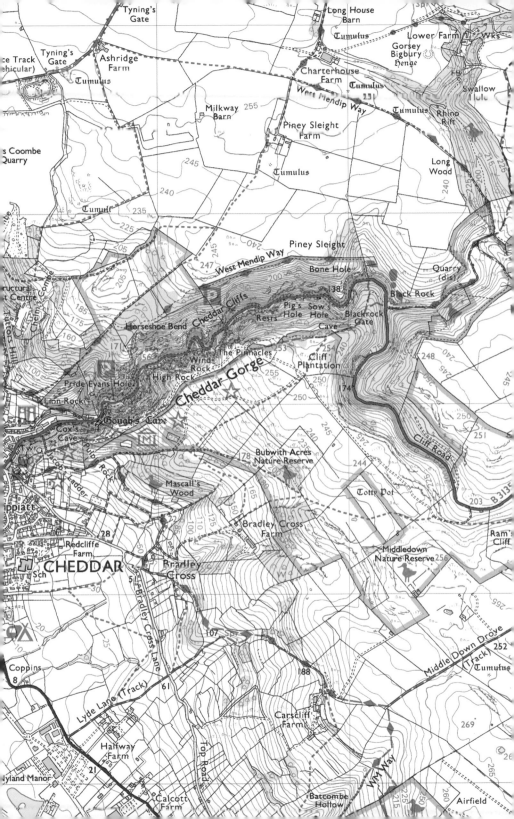

⌀Map 3 PRESELI HILLS

'This makes me somewhat of a historical hippo, you know.'

We were staring at a jutting outcrop of dark rock framed by gorse, and for a while I was confused. I turned to Aunt Bea, raising my eyebrow.

'Well, most people would go to Stonehenge. If we want to talk about our Neolithic ancestors. World-famous landmark, good parking. So why am I taking you here to a corner of wonderfully hilly Pembrokeshire? Aside from the marvellous scenery, which we shall be setting out into shortly. It's a bit left field isn't it.' Aunt Bea was clearly proud of herself.

'Ah, I think you mean hipster.'

'That's what I said. Anyway, look at that stone; it fractures naturally like that. It almost looks like scales, but when we get closer, you can see the odd stump at the base. Stone was quarried here, by our Neolithic ancestors with stone and wood and bone tools. They would have hammered in wedges and then split the pieces of stone away.

'We know that stone from here made its way almost 200 miles away to Stonehenge in Wiltshire. The majority of the big stones, the sarsens, come from within 20 miles. But the smaller inner circle, the bluestones came from Wales, and at least one of them came from right here.

'Just think about that, my boy. Stonehenge is a wonder we've become somewhat used to. But I think seeing the stone here; thinking about those people thousands of years ago, prising the stone from the hillside. Nobody knows why it had to be this type of stone. Perhaps because of how it sounds when you hit it against something? They're said to have a ringing quality. Perhaps this place has some sacred connection we no longer know about. For whatever reason, people dragged these two-tonne stones for hundreds of miles. The Neolithic period is the time, all across the world, when farming has begun to reshape how we lived. In this part of the world, we were very much not early adopters where agriculture was concerned by the way – in the Middle East and Greece it had been a way of life for thousands of years and it was then brought over here by travellers to these shores. For many in the modern world, the essence of a traditional sense of these islands is a cultivated field. But again the reality is much more interesting. Just a bit further up this track, then we'll turn around. Just time for some puzzles, I think.'

■ Easy

1. How many fords are marked on the map?

2. Which full or partial grid section has the highest surveyed point, starting with 1A at the top left, numbers increasing downwards and letters increasing to the right?

■ Medium

3. Which location name contains the most letters, ignoring punctuation?

4. What name printed on the map sounds like an instruction to take care of some financial matters?

■ Tricky

5. From the cattle grid, is it further to Tafarn-y-bwlch or the peak of Foel Cwmcerwyn as the crow flies?

6. If you go directly from the centre of the smallest number on the map to the spring nearest to it, how many contour lines do you pass through?

■ Challenging

7. Which two place names can be combined to form the anagram FRENCH PASTA CYNIC?

8. The following block of simple cipher text identifies four locations on the map.

   DBTUFMMZDZOIFO

   CXMDIQFOOBOU

   NZOZEEEVDPNNJO

   TUBOEJOHTUPOFT

Can you identify them?

Romans

Map 4 PEGWELL BAY

'Not surprisingly, my boy, a lot happened over the next several thousand years.'

We were looking out over a wide, shallow bay, the wind whipping the loose sand up in billows.

'The spread of new technologies and culture. Communities working with Bronze and then Iron Age tools, as our ancestors became ever more settled and cleared more and more of the forests for crops and livestock. The countryside is studded with their tools and implements. Remember, of course, there was no unified country or nation. A myriad of tribes existed across a patchwork of territories. We could have taken a trip to any number of fascinating sites where evidence of settlements from those years remain. Perhaps next time we will. But quite frankly, time marches swiftly onwards.'

'I have been impatient to get to this moment. The moment in the summer of 54 BC when looking out over the bay we would have seen an enormous fleet of Roman ships.'

Looking out over the water, I could easily imagine the horizon teeming with ships and almost shivered.

'Caesar had been here the year before but he'd only brought two legions, and though he landed, soon set off again. It was somewhat of a minor detour in his seven-year campaign against the Gauls. This time he brought

hundreds of ships, some say twenty thousand men and thousands of horses. The weather was terrible with a storm blowing up, and the ships at anchor were broken against themselves. So they pulled the ships up on to the beach. Archaeologists have found evidence of the defensive fortifications the Romans made to defend the ships less than a kilometre in that direction.'

Aunt Bea pointed inland. 'They found pottery and iron weapons, including crucially a Roman spear. Back then, this would all have been an island, cut off from the mainland by the Wantsum Channel until it gradually silted up over the next thousand years. The watching tribes fled at the size of the force. Caesar won some victories over the various tribes that Britain was made up of and left again. But that initial link had been made between here and the Roman world. Over the next eighty years, there were many planned invasions, including my favourite story, of Caligula gathering a force of 200,000 only for them to collect seashells. It wasn't until AD 40 that the invasion began in earnest and for the next forty years vicious battles were waged as the Romans sought to subdue the various tribes.

'This had thus far been an island that had been shaped by those who came to its shores. But no one could have had any idea quite what that fleet signified on that stormy summer day. Now, I think some puzzles.'

■ Easy

1. How many clubhouses are marked on the map?

2. What location name is nearest to the lowest road survey height on the map?

■ Medium

3. How many different road numbers appear on the map?

4. Which location sounds like it might be a storage battery?

■ Tricky

5. Which of the following numbers are printed on the map: 3, 9, 18, 23, 52?

6. How many times do the letters ELL appear next to each other on the map?

■ Challenging

7. With respect to the map, which of the following is the odd one out: WELL, SITE, CROSS, CLUB, POINT?

8. Can you piece these fragments back together to make four locations shown on the map: BOR, BURY, CAN, DITI, ENSC, ONAL, ORE, OUGH, RICH, SEV, TER, TRA.

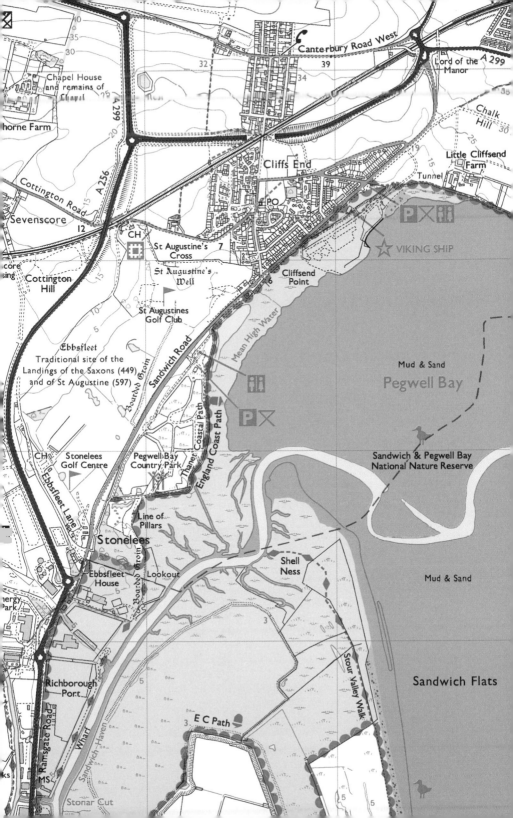

Canterbury Road West

Lord of the Manor

A 299

Chalk Hill

Little Cliffsend Farm

Tunnel

Chapel House and remains of Chapel

thorne Farm

A 299

Cliffs End

PO

Sevenscore

Cottington Road

A 256

CH

St Augustine's Cross

St Augustine's Well

VIKING SHIP

Cliffsend Point

Mean High Water

Cottington Hill

St Augustines Golf Club

Ebbsfleet
Traditional site of the Landings of the Saxons (449) and of St Augustine (597)

Bourbeo Groin

Sandwich Road

Mud & Sand

Pegwell Bay

CH

Stonelees Golf Centre

Pegwell Bay Country Park

Thanet Coastal Path

England Coast Path

Sandwich & Pegwell Bay National Nature Reserve

Ebbsfleet Lane

Line of Pillars

Stonelees

Bourbeo Groin

Lookout

Shell Ness

Mud & Sand

Ebbsfleet House

nergy Park

Stour Valley Walk

Richborough Port

Wharf

Sandwich Flats

Ramsgate Road

E C Path

Sandwich-Haven

MS

Stonar Cut

Map 5 NORWICH CASTLE

'If you want something done properly, my advice is: ask a woman.'

We were looking up at the impressively neat cube of Norwich Castle towering over us and the city around us.

'It looks so neat because it was refaced with Bath stone in the nineteenth century, but reportedly the work was based closely on the medieval design, which itself was on the site where William the Conqueror built his fort. However more important to us is that we believe that this was the site of a fort held by the Iceni tribe.'

Bea left a pause but I made a gesture for her to continue.

'The Iceni were one of the many tribes around the islands that were forced to pay tribute to the Romans after they arrived. They were nominally allowed to keep many of their customs and laws but were effectively under occupation. When the king of the Iceni died, the Romans forcibly annexed his kingdom. It was his wife Boudicca who raised a rebellion throughout East Anglia. The account from a contemporary historian called Tacitus tell us that a total of 70,000 Romans and Britons who supported the Romans were killed. And she reportedly wiped out a whole Roman legion.'

Even I had to admit that was pretty impressive.

'We don't really know a huge amount for sure about Boudicca. All that chariot with blades coming out of the wheels stuff is nonsense. And she's definitely not buried under King's Cross Station. But there are contemporary accounts of her as tall and fierce and the Romans were clearly terrified of her, with good reason.

'If we have time there's a beautiful walk south towards a town called Diss, which is essentially in the footsteps of her army. Boudicca is often held up as a classic example of British rebellion against tyranny. However, I always think it's important to keep in mind that other very English tradition of quietly following the rules that many other tribes were part of! Eventually she died, but we don't know precisely how. But I prefer to think of her as a reminder of how central to the history of Britain women are, though they have often gone recorded. The next lot of puzzles please.'

QUESTIONS

■ Easy

1. Where is the most westerly footbridge on the map?

2. Which location includes the name of a farm animal?

■ Medium

3. Where on the map would you find an irregular heptagon?

4. Which of the three columns of the map grid – left, centre or right – contains the fewest marked places of worship?

■ Tricky

5. Which route on the map would be suitable for the entrance of a Celtic conqueror?

6. Which of the following roads is the odd one out: A146, A147, A1151 or A1242?

■ Challenging

7. What place on the map contains a word that is one letter change away from a word for the residents of a dwelling?

8. Take the largest road number on the map and add 2. Divide the result by the number of museums shown, and from that result, subtract both the highest ground survey height (black point and accompanying number) and the lowest aerial survey height (orange point and accompanying number). What is the result?

Map 6 BENNACHIE

'If there was going to be one part of the country that caused the Romans most trouble, it was always going to be that most tenacious northerly bit.'

I knew that Aunt Bea was very proud of the Scottish part of our ancestry and never missed a reference to it. We were walking along a woodland path, with the sound of birds far above us as we breathed in that unique cool still air in a forest.

'The south had settled most quickly into relative stability, though the Romans still needed large numbers of troops stationed there to keep order. The Romans hadn't expected it to take so long, but thanks to Boudicca and other uprisings in Wales and northern England, it wasn't until the autumn of AD 83 that they prepared for the battle that would represent their conquering of the most northerly point of Britain. After forty years of brutal fighting, this would mark the moment the Romans could say they had conquered the far north of this island. We're not entirely sure where they met, but we think it's most likely that it was just to the north of the Bennachie hills. In the end it was a resounding victory for the Romans with records showing they lost only 300 men, with the Scottish tribes losing at least twenty times that many troops.

'There have been many stories to explain the distinctive shape of the Bennachie hills, one of which being that it was giants and devils who shaped the land by throwing boulders in fits of temper.

'The Romans ended up returning south and gave up the difficult lands to the north to the native tribes. Scottish culture grew up separate but entwined with its southern neighbour. It would be wrong to caricature them as the fierce northern neighbours though. There was a fascinating separate culture in Scotland and a complex relationship between those north of the border and those south of it that was to be a relationship that echoed over the next two thousand years. We could spend a lifetime exploring the history of Scotland, my boy. There are a huge number of extremely important historical sites, and for my money it is the most beautiful country in the world. There's something about the mixture of stone and water, grass and heather, which can't help but call to your soul. I think there's a break in the trees not too far ahead. We can stop there and look at the next lot of puzzles.'

■ Easy

1. What facilities are available at the parking place?

2. What is the highest point on the map?

■ Medium

3. What location shares its name with a popular political concept regarding the acceptable range of political opinion?

4. Which full or partial grid section contains the largest number of words, starting with 1A at the top left, numbers increasing downwards and letters increasing to the right?

■ Tricky

5. Where would you find the digits 1, 1 and 6 together on the map, but in a different order?

6. With respect to the map, which of the following is the odd one out: BURN, POT, TAP?

■ Challenging

7. The 250m contour line that passes Scarfauld Hill circles around which other elevated location?

8. What elevation is the contour line that passes through the 'o' of Braes o' Bennachie?

Map 7 HADRIAN'S WALL

'A marker of just how worried by the resolute northern tribes the Romans were can be seen here in the creation of one of the most famous walls in the world.'

We were walking through the dappled shade of a pretty churchyard. Aunt Bea stopped walking and gestured with her arm.

'About five miles in that direction, north, is Gretna Green, famous in later years as the place where young couples would come to take advantage of the more relaxed Scottish laws around marriage, being the easiest place in Scotland to get to.'

Aunt Bea knelt down to look at a gravestone.

'People often assume that the wall maps on to the current border between England and Scotland, but in fact it stretched for over 70 miles from Bowness-on-Solway just to the west of us to Wallsend in the east, near Newcastle. Like a necktie across the collar of the country. Later they would build a more northerly turf fortification up between the Firth of Forth and the Firth of Clyde, but it only lasted eight years before they retreated back south to here again.'

'There's a monument to Edward I somewhere round here too, whose warlike relationship with our neighbours to the north would echo the Romans' over a thousand years later. There are other stretches of the wall that are more visible of course, and one day we must visit some of them, but the reason I'm so very interested in this particular stretch of wall is the fort that once stood here that the Romans knew as Aballava. In 1934, they discovered a stone with Latin carved into it which described a group of soldiers known as "the Aurelian Moors" who had been stationed there. We know there would have been a whole community around the fort, including the soldiers' families. It is the first recorded African community in Britain. And our sense of just how racially diverse Romans in Britain were is increasing all the time. The famous "Ivory Bangle Lady" was a skeleton dating from the third century, who was from a North African background and of a high social class. The greatest gift that comes from looking into the past with clear eyes is that it reframes our understanding of now and, with any luck, the future. Now what say you we sit here for a while and crack on with a few more of our clues?'

▇ Easy

1. What is the total of the numbers in the map grid square that contains the 28m road survey height?

2. Where on the map would you find the letters LEG near the letters ARM?

▇ Medium

3. Which place shares a name with a famous district of London?

4. Heading precisely west from the 12m aerial survey height near Hill Farm, how many black lines do you pass through before hitting the edge of the map?

▇ Tricky

5. Which location is one letter change from being a location where witches might gather?

6. With respect to the map, which of the following is the odd one out: LONG, MARSH, MOOR, SANDS?

▇ Challenging

7. Can you find locations on the map that are anagrams of the following words or phrases? Ignore the spaces and punctuation, which may differ from those in the place names.
   a. ELECT ISLAM   c. FEARED LIMB
   b. HOGGIN' DRUIDS   d. HAM WEATHERING

8. Head directly north from the school building until your path intersects a number. Turn left, and keep going to the second footpath. Head south along that footpath, without turning off, until you reach its end. Move directly south-west from that point until you pass the end of a piece of woodland split by a path. What place name is immediately south of you on the map?

Groynes

Burghmarsh Point

Mean High Water

Groyne.

Old Sandsfield

King Edward 1st Monument

7

12

Channel of River Eden

Ridding Sough

NTL

FB

10

75

Burgh Marsh

20

NTL

25

27

Butts (dis)

18

22

Ridding Sough

Watch Hill

21

FBs

MILECASTLE 73

25

Dykesfield

TURRET 72B

Sewage Works

Burgh by Sands

North End

ABALLAVA ROMAN FORT

HADRIAN'S WALL (course of)

HADRIAN'S WALL (course of)

VALLUM (course of)

PO

13

Hadrian's Wall Path

Longburgh Farm

West End

Amberfield

Sch.

Longburgh

Station Cottages

19

Hill Farm

12

Shield

20

22

28

25

18

29

Shield Farm

Burgh Moor House

20

21

Well d

16

24

urghmoor Wood

31

30

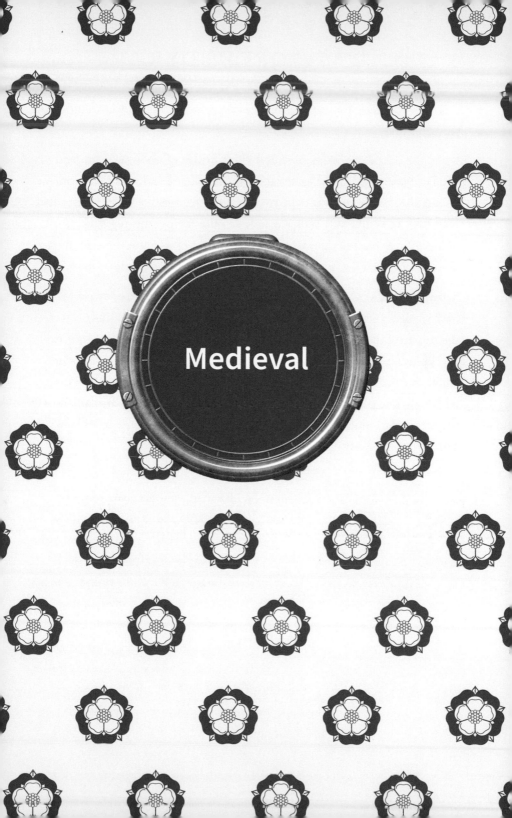

Medieval

Map 8 OFFA'S DYKE

'Another boundary for us to ruminate on, my boy. This one from a different period entirely.'

Up to the left of us was an incredible folded ridge of earth, as if the land had been bunched up like material. In the distance I saw hills rising and falling, the dark line of the dyke tracing the land ahead of us. Aunt Bea had promised we would only walk a couple of miles before turning back. But I didn't entirely trust her not to sneak the entire 177 miles past me as she had already told me it was one of her favourite walks in the whole of the country.

'Clawdd Offa, or Offa's Dyke. Magnificent isn't it. Of course, we could have spent several years, just solidly touring Roman sites in Britain. Over the course of their almost 400 years on this island it was changed forever, and there are so many places to study, from the baths of Bath to Chester's amphitheatre. If you find a long straight road on a map, the odds are that it's based on an old Roman one. Roman Britain came to an end formally in AD 410 when the emperor Honorius famously replied for a request for help with a message effectively saying "sort yourselves out".'

Aunt Bea expounded on how with the Romans out of the way, the following centuries saw waves of invasion by Germanic people, including Jutes from Jutland, which is part of Denmark now, Angles from the south of Denmark and Saxons from Germany, with the formation of separate and warring kingdoms, which comprised Northumbria, Mercia, East Anglia, Essex, Kent, Sussex and Wessex. In the middle of this in AD 595, St Augustine was sent by Pope Gregory to convert the pagan island to Christianity.

'The earthworks we're walking alongside is thought to have acted as a border between Mercia, Offa's Christian, Anglo-Saxon kingdom and the Welsh kingdom of Powys. There would almost certainly have been forts along its length. Offa was a bellicose fellow, who famously had other kings killed, including his son-in-law. His name is well known because of this spectacular construction and he was clearly an impressive leader to have accomplished such a feat of construction as well as conquering many of the neighbouring kingdoms.'

Bees hummed in and out of the blackberry bushes.

'I love this place, I think, because it reminds me of how things that feel so certain at the time can disappear. Our own sense of what it is to be British is so recent. The great kingdom of Mercia, so sure of itself, and its ability to build this astonishing feat of engineering. I am yet to meet a proud Mercian in my lifetime. I think just another couple of miles and then we'll turn back. If I remember rightly there's a splendid old oak tree not too far ahead. We shall sit under it and solve our next lot of clues.'

■ Easy

1. How many times does the word 'Tumulus' appear on the map?

2. Where is the highest spring on the map?

■ Medium

3. Which location is the nearest as the crow flies to the most northerly end of Offa's Dyke Path on the map?

4. Which of the complete map grid squares shows the flattest terrain?

■ Tricky

5. Including 'plantation', how many different, complete English words printed on the map are directly associated with vegetation?

6. Which location sounds like it might have enjoyed the 1970s?

■ Challenging

7. In a woodland that surrounds a castle, follow the path north to its terminus. Jump to the nearest well, and follow its footpath to a place of worship. Move to the nearest orange road and head west to a telephone. There is a ground survey point nearby. Jump to another ground survey point that is exactly four metres different in height to the one you are currently at. Which named location is south-west of your position?

8. Make a note of each of the following six numerical values observed from the map:

   a. The second highest survey point

   b. The number of letters in the longest location name

   c. The number of times the word 'Burfa' appears

   d. The number of named farms

   e. The lowest height printed on the map

   f. The number of wells shown

   Using each of these six numbers exactly once, performing only the elemental mathematical operations – addition, subtraction, multiplication and division – can you arrive at a total of exactly 300?

Map 9 YORK

'Welcome, my boy, to Jorvik!'

My aunt was standing in the centre of the pavement with her arms outstretched. People ducked under her arms to move past. I winced and gently tugged her to the side.

'A Roman fortress town, this had already become a thriving city by the ninth century, when the rather marvellously named Viking, Ivar the Boneless arrived, captured it and made it the capital of their northern territory. The Norse word for street is 'gate', giving a rather wonderful literal quality to their street names. One's called Swinegate, which was a lane where pigs were kept and my personal favourite Whip-Ma-Whop-Ma-Gate, which is a street where punishment by whipping was doled out.'

We were wandering through winding cobbled streets, with a pleasingly jumbled wooden-fronted building leaning down over us, and Aunt Bea excitedly jabbing her finger at things that caught her attention.

'This was a street of butchers, and these channels were to wash the blood and offal away. Ah, but that won't be for another six hundred years yet!'

I steered her gently away from a group of tourists in case they thought she was a guide.

'York would be under Viking rule for almost a hundred years. In the popular imagination, we think of Vikings as pointy-helmeted marauders, mainly notable for their boats, battle and pillage, which I'll admit they did a fair bit of. But under their rule, Jorvik was to become a key commercial and trading centre. Remember, this was a period of constant battles between the pagan Viking invaders and the Christian Anglo-Saxons, the most famously pious of which, Alfred the Great, had a dream to unify the various kingdoms into one. Alfred died without seeing it but in AD 927 his grandson Athelstan annexed York and succeeded for the first time in ruling a unified kingdom we would recognise as England. That wasn't the end of things, of course – there was still time for Alfred's descendants to negotiate the kingdom away to Canute, the king of the North Sea Empire, for twenty years, then another descendant to win it back. And if I tell you that this particular pious chap, known as Edward the Confessor, had a Norman mother, I think you'll have an inkling of what's to come. What is it you young people say; "spoilers"?'

Aunt Bea peered around, blinking. 'Now you rummage around in that bag and find the next lot of puzzles we need to look at and I'll try and remember where that shop with the amazing Pontefract cakes is.'

Easy

1. Where are the islands shown on the map?

2. What is the height of the aerial survey point?

Medium

3. Which country's name appears on the map?

4. Which location shares a name with a location in each of London, Glasgow and Dublin?

Tricky

5. If you were to travel in a straight line from the bottom left corner of the map to the top right corner, how many coloured roads would you cross?

6. The Jorvik Viking Centre, indicated on the map but not named, is a museum that is immediately adjacent to a place of worship with a spire, minaret or dome. Where is it?

Challenging

7. How many location names printed on the map contain the letters A, C and R adjacent but in any order?

8. Can you piece these fragments back together to make four locations shown on the map: CLE, HOS, IUM, MEN, NAT, OFT, PIT, RCR, RPE, SCA, THO, URE?

Map 10 BATTLE

'The history around some places isn't clear from just a name on a map and must be gently teased out. Some are a little more obvious.'

Aunt Bea looked at me expectantly as we stood in a field dotted with wildflowers, with spreading oak trees in the background. We were strolling slowly towards a sprawling stone abbey and it might have been my imagination but I thought I could smell the tang of sea salt in the air.

I'd seen the name on the road sign as we'd turned off. 'Come on. Even I know which one this is,' I said.

'My faith in the youth of today is restored. Of course, the story of the Battle of Hastings, or at least Harold and the arrow in his eye is one of the most famous stories in British history. Images in the style of the Bayeux Tapestry are a visual shortcut to the very idea of history itself.'

She pointed out a particularly beautiful yellow butterfly.

'After Edward the Confessor died, there was a succession crisis with both Harald the king of Norway and William the Duke of Normandy both laying claim. It turns out invading armies are like buses. William looked like he would invade, so Harald did. Harold marched his armies around 200 miles north from London to Stamford Bridge near York, routed Harald, then marched another 270 miles down to Sussex and met William – a bit like an eleventh-century ultramarathon for warring monarchs. To be honest, I can excuse Harold for being a bit tired by the time he came down and his army was defeated by William's.'

Aunt Bea explained how after William had conquered, he set in place a great era of monastery and cathedral building all across the country, also leaving time for an entire inventory of the country called the Domesday Book.

'The Normans left an indelible mark on these islands, in the cathedrals and the sites of their castles. But perhaps my favourite legacy is in our language, where the names for some animals when they're alive have their roots in the older English forms – pig, cow, sheep; but the word for them when served at a table relates to the French – pork, beef, mutton. All this talk of food is making me hungry. Let's get back to the puzzles, shall we?'

■ Easy

1. What is the lowest aerially surveyed height printed on the map?

2. How many footbridges are indicated on the map?

■ Medium

3. What is the sum total of the different A- and B-road numbers shown on the map?

4. With respect to the map, what do BANK, BARN, PARK and ICE have in common?

■ Tricky

5. The circle that has its centre at the southerly 98m ground survey height and passes through the northerly 98m ground survey height also passes through which nine-letter location name?

6. Using only the initial letters of complete words in the names of farms on the map, can you find a species of ungulate mammal?

■ Challenging

7. Head north from the museum to a windmill. There is an adjacent triangulation pillar. Move to the aerial survey height that is 10m greater. Follow the road westwards to a ground survey height and then head directly westwards to the first spring. If you go south from that point, what is the first location you come to?

8. Can you find locations on the map that are anagrams of the following words or phrases? Ignore the spaces and punctuation, which may differ from those in the place names.

   a. MELTED WHIRLPOOLS

   b. ANY QUOTED SORROW

   c. LETHAL NAME

   d. ANGLOPHILE DETONATORS

Map 11 OXFORD

'"And that sweet city with her dreaming spires. She needs not June for beauty's heightening." Matthew Arnold nailed it there all right.'

Oxford was clearly a place used to this sort of thing, as nobody batted an eyelid when Aunt Bea declaimed into the morning air with her familiar booming poetry voice.

'Oxford had been settled by the Saxons. In one of the easier to parse names, it was known as a particularly good place to ford oxen. There's no real agreed date of foundation of the university, and some date teaching there from as early as 1096, but things really kicked off when Henry II banned English students from attending the University of Paris in 1167. A teensy bit of context; William's son, William – the limited naming imaginations of the monarchs will be a running thread, my boy – succeeded him until he was mysteriously shot on a hunt – oh for a CSI New Forest – and so his brother Henry was named king. He was by all accounts a sensible, capable chap. There's a classic bit of argy-bargy between the Norman barons over his possessions in Normandy. There was a sensitivity about sending all of the best and brightest off to Paris constantly.'

We were walking past the most amazing selection of real-life Hogwarts buildings, and she was calling out words as we went: 'Jericho, Magdalene, Corpus Christi, Brasenose.'

'You must be making that last one up, I remarked.'

'It seems strange to us, not that Oxford and its spires are such a part of the establishment

but that Oxford has always had a rebellious heart to it. In the fourteenth century it was one of the most violent places to be in the world. Just over forty years after 1167, a group of scholars fleeing religious persecution founded Cambridge University. The two remain intertwined with a healthy rivalry, which finds watery expression every year in the Boat Race. Now, I would imagine if you solve this next lot of puzzles, they might even let you study here in the future.'

Easy

1. How many times do the letters FB, indicating a footbridge, appear in the leftmost column of the map's grid squares?

2. How many streams, brooks and canals are named on the map?

Medium

3. Which three road numbers add together to give you a total of 5,395?

4. Which is further from the centre of the star indicating the Ice Rink: the 61m ground survey point on the A420 or the 63m ground survey point on the A4158?

Tricky

5. Which word appearing more than once on the map is one letter away from a term for a professional criminal?

6. Which martyred saint associated with a popular type of firework is named on the map?

Challenging

7. Which two locations on the map combine to form the anagram ENJOY HEROICS?

8. The following block of simple cipher text identifies four locations on the map:
   RUOBRA HDLOCL LAHTER
   AGRAMY DALLLE WREHCR
   EVIRHC TIDERC AGOHZA

Can you identify them?

Map 12 RUNNYMEDE

'For a place of such momentous import, I am always struck by the relatively unassuming nature of this particular spot.'

Aunt Bea and I were eating cake and drinking tea at a picnic table outside a neat brick tea room. Earlier we'd taken a stroll along the bank of the River Thames, almost unrecognisable sleeved with green as it made its way through fields dotted with yellow flowers.

'There's a memorial for President John F. Kennedy and the Allied Air Forces of the Second World War, which we will go and see shortly, but it's Magna Carta we're here for.

'Magna Carta is invoked often, any time someone wants to give their arguments for freedom some heft. You'd need a legal historian to fill you in on all the details, but in the popular imagination, Magna Carta is where we date modern democracy from. It was effectively part of a treaty between King John and the figures who sat just below the king in the feudal hierarchy known as the barons, who were rebelling against his rules. It was, for the

first time in the country, a document that set out the rights and freedoms of "free men" and bound the king to be subject to the rule of law. It would be fair to say that prior to this, most monarchs' attitude towards following rules was limited at best and involved a broad interpretation of the divine right of the monarch. This was King John by the way who often features in the Robin Hood films. It includes things now that are fundamental principles of our society and the roots of democracy.'

It was odd because, as Aunt Bea said, Runnymede wasn't a place that announced itself loudly. But walking through the fields that afternoon, there was a sense that the land had soaked up a huge amount of history. It was incredible to see so many different countries around the world paying homage to the importance of what happened in this field.

'It wasn't as if someone flicked a switch overnight of course and those rights were suddenly available to everyone. But from the principles of Magna Carta flows not only our own Parliament, but also the US Constitution and Bill of Rights and many other nations around the world. Now look sharp, there are clues to solve.'

■ Easy

1. How many unique road numbers are shown on the map?

2. Where would you find a famous American named on the map?

■ Medium

3. If you head directly north from the highest surveyed point on the map, what is the last location name you pass through before leaving the map?

4. Which full or partial grid row contains the greatest number of ground or aerial survey heights?

■ Tricky

5. What facility which comes under 'tourist and leisure' is most common on the map?

6. Where on the map can you find a building in the shape of a squared-off number greater than 1?

■ Challenging

7. With respect to the map, which of the following is the odd one out: SLOPES, MAGNA, FOSTERS, RUNNYMEDE, WHITEHALL, HILL?

8. How many unique examples are there of words on the map which are also common verbs in the infinitive form (i.e. 'Enjoy', 'Wash', 'Run', etc.)?

Map 13 ELDERSLIE

'Just promise me you're not going to start shouting "freedom".'

Aunt Bea had already explained that the reason we were standing looking at a monument in a neat commuter village in west central Scotland was because of the Scottish freedom fighter William Wallace.

There had been strong links between France and Scotland as far back as the eleventh century, but in 1295 they signed something that came to be known as 'The Auld Alliance', an agreement that if either of them were attacked by the English, the other would invade their territory.

'When Edward I of England forcibly manoeuvred himself on to the Scottish throne in 1296, there was immediate unrest in Scotland. We know very little about William, other than he was likely born into the gentry, but we do know he attacked and killed the English sheriff of Lanark the following year and this lit the touchpaper for a full rebellion. Within months he had won a famous victory over the English at the Battle of Stirling Bridge. Over the coming years he played cat and mouse with the English, drawing them deep into Scotland until he was defeated and fled to France. While he was away, the other key Scottish figures came to a truce with the English and a price was put on Wallace's head. When he returned to Scotland, he was captured, brought to London and executed in a famously barbaric way. Let's just say it's never a good thing when they can show off parts of you in five different cities.'

'Wallace has become a symbol of standing up against tyranny. We're about twenty miles south of Loch Lomond, which crosses the Highland boundary fault, the geological feature that separates the Highlands of Scotland from the Lowlands. It's easy to see the history when you're standing in front of a grand castle, but it's all around us. Every morning when these families are eating their breakfast cereal, they are living in the shadow of a man who bent history to his will and inspired many generations.

Now, feel free to get the next set of clues.'

QUESTIONS

■ Easy

1. How many times does the word 'Farm' appear on the map?
2. Which Hill is nearest to the edge of the map?

■ Medium

3. How many places of worship are shown on the map?
4. Where is the highest woodland named on the map?

■ Tricky

5. Where on the map can you find the name of a scientist famous for his work on gravity?
6. The circle which has its centre at the triangulation pillar south-east of Leitchland Farm and passing through the disused shaft north of Wester Craigenfeoch also passes through which four-letter location identifier printed on the map?

■ Challenging

7. From a mast near a tidal limit, head westwards to a large roundabout and head directly south until between a school and a fire station. Head east to another school, then north to a B-road. Turn east to the next junction. Turn south there and follow the road past two junctions with coloured roads, then take the second right. Where are you?
8. Add the number of schools shown to the number of times the word 'Weir' or 'Weirs' appears, and subtract 1. Divide the total into ten less than the first ground survey height to the north of Glenpatrick, and multiply the result by the highest contour line elevation printed on the map. Add one less than the eastern-most triangulation pillar height, and divide this by the result of subtracting the number of Park and Ride facilities from the lowest aerial survey height. What is the result?

Map 14 WEYMOUTH

'Sometimes history turns on the very biggest of things. Sometimes on something no bigger than a flea.'

We were looking out over a busy harbour with multicoloured boats, their masts angled against each other against the pale blue sky.

'There had already been an outbreak of plague in the sixth and seventh centuries known as the Plague of Justinian, with some estimates saying that as much as half of the population of Europe was wiped out. It hit especially hard in the Kingdom of Powys, on the Welsh side of Offa's Dyke. It reappeared some time in 1346 with the first definitive case in Crimea in 1347. But in June 1348, when a seaman bedded down on the north side of the harbour after docking from Gascony, it was to signal the arrival of a new wave of plague that killed at least a quarter of the population of Britain. We now know it was a bacteria spread by the Oriental rat flea and it spread rapidly through the south-west of the country, as people fleeing from the plague brought it inland, before it reached London the following year.'

It seemed so odd to be listening to such misery with the cheerful clanking of boats rigging all around us and the familiar sound of gulls.

'It had a mortality rate of over 50 per cent, and in the cramped conditions of fourteenth century cities and towns it spread with horrifying speed. Over the next five years it's estimated that it wiped out 30 to 60 per cent of Europe's entire population. It left a legacy for generations, as people ascribed the devastation to a God angry at their behaviour and lashed out at scapegoats. It took generations for the global population to approach anything like it had been. There is a school of thought that it freed peasants from their traditional obligation to remain on the land known as serfdom and it led to higher wages for skilled labourers. Some believe it even finds expression in the nursery rhyme Ring-a-Ring o' Roses.

'There is such history in Britain's coasts. It hardly needs pointing out that we're an island, but there are such adventures to be found at the points at which people and ideas left and entered the country. Those can be stories of celebration, but in this instance one of lamentation. Now, perhaps a little too much sadness for such a pretty day. Distract me with a puzzle or two.'

■ Easy

1. Which location sounds like a nasty garbage-related accident?

2. Where would you find a school next to a cemetery?

■ Medium

3. How many locations on the map are specifically associated with fish?

4. How many places are there on the map that allow you to hide?

■ Tricky

5. Which route is named after a celebrated Wessex author?

6. Which is further from the Wyke Regis post office, the Landing Stage or the Town Bridge?

■ Challenging

7. How many times does the diphthong vowel 'ou' appear on the map?

8. Can you find locations on the map that are anagrams of the following words or phrases? Ignore the spaces and punctuation, which may differ from those in the place names.
   a. MESMERIC GLOBE
   b. AND COOLS FASTEST
   c. WHAT CHASTE OUTPOSTS
   d. RECIPROCAL MIME

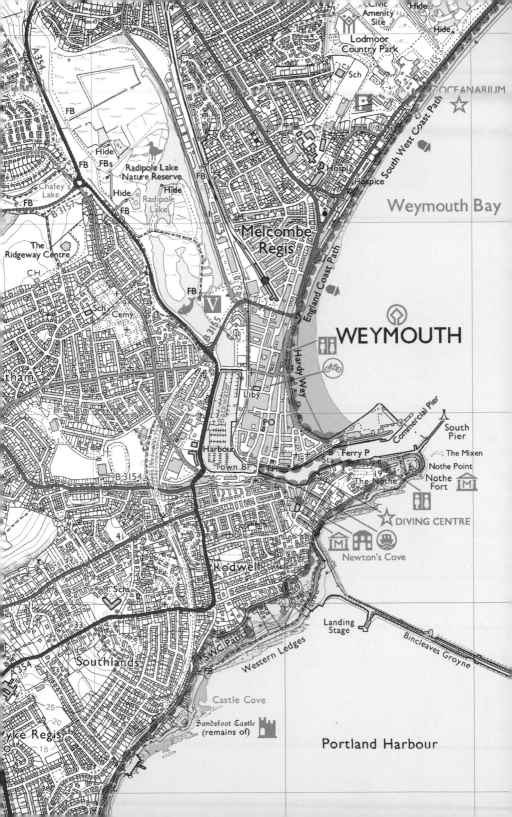

Tudors

Map 15 WESTMINSTER

'Bacteria can spread with astonishing speed, but so too can ideas.'

We were walking alongside the Thames path, groups of pink-faced joggers in bright outfits parting around us. Across the river from us were the filigreed buildings of Parliament and Big Ben shining in the sunlight.

'We're leaping forwards here now, my boy, accelerating all the time. Forgive me if I skip some Henrys and the Wars of the Roses on this trip after so much recent death. There's too much, too much history for us to fit in. The headlines were: lots of warring with the French, lots of warring within the House of Plantagenet. All incredibly important and of course ultimately ushers in that famous bunch, the Tudors, but as I say, too much blood for me. And besides, I find the pen is both mightier and more interesting than the sword.'

We sat at a bench and watched the boats passing down the iconic River Thames.

'It was of course the German Johannes Gutenberg who began experimenting with the technology for printing in 1440, and by 1450 set up the world's first commercial press. But it was a merchant called William Caxton who brought that technology to these shores and set up a press in Westminster in 1475.

'By modern standards it was laborious, with each page needing to be set up with metal type, but prior to that the only way of copying texts was by hand – the word manuscript is literally the Latin for 'written by hand'. A single printing press could print thousands of pages a day, many hundreds of times what a team of scribes could produce. The press led to books becoming massively cheaper and more available to everyone. Without this technology, our entire history would be unimaginably different, and the printing press has grounds to be one of the most transformative technologies in the history of mankind. It is impossible to imagine what the world would have been like without it. Now, let's take a stroll by the river and you can read out some clues to me.'

■ Easy

1. How many libraries are specifically indicated on the map?

2. Where on the map could you be in the audience of an international cricket match?

■ Medium

3. The word 'Mayfair' appears on the map. What does it mean?

4. What do you get if you add the number of bridges named on the map to the number of museums shown (excluding art galleries)?

■ Tricky

5. With respect to the map, which of these is the odd one out: Banqueting, Lancaster, Leicester, Somerset?

6. Where is the largest complete island shown on the map?

■ Challenging

7. Can you piece these fragments back together to make four locations shown on the map: ALF, ARL, BAT, DBR, ENT, ERS, ESTI, FOR, GER, HALL, HOU, HUN, IAM, IDGE, ION, OFP, POW, ROY, SEA, SES, TAT, TER, VAL?

8. Using only pink capital letters in the names of Tube stations, can you find an eight-letter word meaning 'clean'?

Map 16 LINLITHGOW

'Becoming Queen of Scotland at six days old is a steep learning curve for anyone, I'd say.'

We were gazing up at the magnificent ruins of Linlithgow Palace, set in neat grass at the edge of a dark loch.

'You may have noticed, my boy, that we've skipped another fair few Henrys, a couple of Edwards and a Richard, too. I can feel the waggy finger of a proper historian as I speak. However there are too many stories and only so much time. I've even left out that biggest box office of all, the larger than life eighth Henry. Traditionally I've always found the English Reformation to be a bit too much about a lot of men shouting at each other – Henry VIII, Pope Clement VII, Cardinal Wolsey then Thomas Cromwell. The entire fabric of a nation torn up by a husband who kept changing wives, as Henry VIII breaks with Rome in order to get a divorce from Catherine of Aragon. However, I have always been rather drawn to the story of the infant queen.

'When Mary's father, the King of Scotland died, Henry VIII, fearing the French were making inroads via Scotland, proposed a marriage between his son, Edward, and Mary. However, the Scots refused and so, in what became known as the 'Rough Wooing', Henry attacked Scotland and demanded that they agree to a marriage between his then six-year-old son Edward and the infant queen. Regents governed Scotland while she grew up in France, and when she was sixteen she was married to the Dauphin, or heir to

the French throne, and became consort when he took the throne. When he died, she returned to Scotland and married her half cousin, Henry Stuart, Lord Darnley and they had a son. The following year, his house blew up and he was found dead in the garden. A man called James Hepburn, the fourth Earl of Bothwell, was the prime suspect, though he was acquitted. So a month later Mary married him. This caused quite the uproar and she was forced to abdicate and flee south in the hope of protection from her cousin Queen Elizabeth.

'Elizabeth was a remarkable woman and monarch, who was able to somehow find a compromise between Roman Catholicism and Protestantism in the Church of England. She would rule for forty-five years and under her reign, Britain would begin a process of discovery that was a precursor to the processes of colonisation and the vast expansion of trade. I have always thought of how hard it must have been to rule as a woman in that time, and of course she and Mary were so very different in every way. I cannot imagine they were particularly fond of each other.

'Unfortunately for Mary, she was considered by many to have the truer claim to the English throne and was therefore a threat. When she was linked to a plot to overthrow the Queen, Elizabeth signed her death warrant. Let us distract ourselves with some more puzzles though.'

■ Easy

1. Where on the map would you find a monument?

2. Which farm on the map has the longest name?

■ Medium

3. Which full or partial row of the map grid contains the most survey height points?

4. Which is further from The Rickle, the centre of the cemetery or Gardners Hall?

■ Tricky

5. With respect to the map, which of the following numbers is the odd one out: 70, 72, 74, 75, 77, 80?

6. Which four numbers printed on the map sum to a total of 1,800?

■ Challenging

7. From the disused mine, follow the road east to a location that shares a name with a district of east London. Head directly south to the next named location, and make a beeline to the nearest coloured road. From the number printed nearby, head south south-east to a train station, and then a little south of west to a nearby T-junction. Head in a south-westerly direction from there to a location that sounds like a sandwich shop. What is the first word printed to the south of your current location?

8. Which two place names on the map combine to make the anagram THE MENACING GLAMOUR?

Map 17 STRATFORD UPON AVON

'Everyone can master a grief but he that has it.'

We were sitting on a bench facing out over the River Avon with the church at our backs and willow trees leaning over the water as if on tiptoes.

'That's a line from *Much Ado About Nothing*. Shakespeare wrote it two or three years after his only son Hamnet died at the age of eleven. We know almost nothing about him, other than his name appears in the parish registry of deaths for this churchyard.

'I cannot pretend Shakespeare is in any way a hidden figure. But he straddles Elizabeth, the last of the Tudor monarchs, and James, the first of the Stuarts. We must always remember that when he was writing his history plays, he was writing plays about the forebears of the Queen. Of course, for many people, what matters is the art. To try and trace links to his life isn't the point to them. But for me, to situate him in time and space, as a grieving father, doesn't minimise the plays. In his words we find so many coordinates we

can map our own lives by. Love and
sadness, wit and dumb feeling.
Later we can head into town
and take a trip through the huge
number of sights. But for some
reason, walking this churchyard,
we can think about him not as a
playwright or a genius who stands
outside of time, but as a grieving
father.'

The shadows were growing
longer and the tall, sharp spire was
beginning to darken against the sky.

'So many layers of history everywhere. There was a church here when this
was Mercia, and the Normans almost certainly built their own stone church.
This church was begun in the thirteenth century, and in this churchyard,
a man who would write plays about so much of Britain's history stood and
grieved, little knowing the astonishing shocks that were to come over the
next hundred years. Let us try some puzzles.'

■ Easy

1. Which location name on the map contains the most letters?

2. Which of the following tourist and leisure sites is not indicated on the map: historic building, picnic site, public house, recreation centre or viewpoint?

■ Medium

3. What is on the second-highest peak shown on the map?

4. Which location on the map sounds like it might be a place for UN peacekeepers to hide?

■ Tricky

5. If you move directly from Temple Hill to the structure in the Playing Fields, how many roads do you cross?

6. If straight lines went from the 33m aerial survey height east of the racecourse to the 39m ground survey height north of the racecourse and on to the 34m aerial survey height within the racecourse, would the angle they formed be greater or lesser than 30 degrees?

■ Challenging

7. How many unabbreviated religious terms are printed on the map?

8. Using only the initial letters of complete words in the names of locations that contain 'Hill' in their name, can you find a nine-letter word for a children's game?

Map 18 PLYMOUTH

'There's a great deal of history in these parts.'

We were walking from a harbour towards somewhere called the Hoe in Plymouth. Another one of those striped red-and-white lighthouses visible in the distance.

'The story is that the Hoe was where Sir Francis Drake was playing bowls when the Spanish Armada was spotted in 1588. But we're in these parts to think about boats leaving, rather than arriving.

'It was from here that a group of Protestants, who felt that the Church of England was forever tainted by its proximity to the Church of Rome and were facing persecution for their beliefs, departed for the New World.

'We've seen Christianity from its first arrival as a cult brought over by the Romans, on through its battle for survival over pagan religions in the time of the Angles, Saxons and Jutes. It rallies with Alfred the Great and his Christian heirs, and is cemented by William the Conqueror's arrival. And relatively speaking, the English are worshipping within the Roman Catholic tradition. We were lagging behind our northern neighbours where a German

professor of theology called Martin Luther was
breaking from Catholic Christian traditions
and establishing a form of worship known
as Protestantism. Its adherents believed
that the Latin services, ornate churches and
associated finery of the Catholic tradition
were unnecessary and that the true form
of worship should be free of the structures and
trappings of the Church. That is a very simple way
of describing what was an enormously complicated
process, of course, and one which transformed the world;
just under forty years before Walter Raleigh had set sail for the New World
and tried and failed to found colonies in The Americas. This was part of
the larger events of the period, known as "the age of discovery", as Europe
explored the world and founded colonies.

'The "pilgrims" set off from Plymouth with 102 passengers bound for
Virginia. However, on the way they were blown off course and landed further
north on the New England coast where they established the first settlement
in the New World and transformed everything for ever. Now, my boy, next
puzzle, please.'

■ Easy

1. Where on the map would you find a strictly seasonal route?

2. Which full or partial column of the map grid contains the most places of worship?

■ Medium

3. How many stations are shown on the map?

4. What species of bird associated with Edgar Alan Poe appears twice on the map?

■ Tricky

5. Barrow Park is a site on the map. In this context, what does 'barrow' mean?

6. Which location's name contains a word that is one letter change away from being a type of fastener?

■ Challenging

7. Starting at the top of the map and staying on coloured roads as if you were driving, take the first left off the B3396, the first right, the third left, turn right, take the second right, and then left. Finally, take the first white road left. Where are you?

8. Which two place names can be combined to form the anagram REMARKABLE MAP CONCEPT?

Stuarts

Map 19 WORCESTER

'Perhaps it is testament to my essentially pacifistic nature that I've chosen the site of its last battle to introduce you to the English Civil War at all, my boy.'

Behind her, Worcester Cathedral rose up over the River Severn, and a white river cruise boat passed us by.

'This battle was in 1651 and would bring to a close nine years of fighting after an extraordinary sequence of events, including the execution of a king and the exile of his heir. It is a peaceful place to think about such a bloody conflict. The battle was between supporters of King Charles II, drawn mainly from Scotland and known as Cavaliers and supporters of Parliament led by Oliver Cromwell known as Roundheads. Two years previously, Charles I had been executed for treason after a fraught and combative relationship with Parliament. After he had married a Catholic there was fear that he wanted to make England a Catholic country. He also constantly dissolved Parliament, meaning he in effect ruled on his own, only recalling Parliament when he needed more money.

'You'll notice this brings together a number of common factors, my boy: tension with Scotland, tension with France and an ever-growing tension over the rights of those who ruled us and the people.

'When the troops led by Cromwell endured, Charles I was executed, his son exiled and Cromwell took over as Lord Protector of the Commonwealth of England, Scotland and Ireland for five years followed by his son. It is fair to say that Cromwell has been a divisive figure, depending on who is judging him. After he died and his son's authority quickly ebbed away, Charles II was reinstated as monarch and had Oliver Cromwell's body dug up and subjected to a posthumous execution, which is not a phrase I have ever had cause to use before. In rather more cheerful news it is the home of a delicious sauce I am rather partial to. Perhaps we could look for somewhere that could do us some cheese on toast topped with it and you can read me out some more of those pesky puzzles.'

■ Easy

1. How many directly touching circular structures are in the largest group of unbroken touching circles at the Sewage Works west of Diglis?

2. What is the greatest height printed on the map?

■ Medium

3. Which individual digit appears the most times on the map?

4. Which sounds like the most colourful location on the map?

■ Tricky

5. Which outlined building on the map looks most like a capital letter?

6. Where can you find the names of creatures on the map?

■ Challenging

7. The following block of simple cipher text identifies four locations on the map.

TNHVDRSHTX

BZRBNTRND

RZCDCNTRSD

MZNNRFZRM

Can you identify them?

8. Can you piece these fragments back together to make four locations shown on the map: ARA, ATH, BRI, BRO, CES, CHC, CHP, CNGD, DEP, DGE, EEC, HOIR, MWI, PIT, ROF, SWAY, TER, THR, TRE, WOR?

Map 20 PUDDING LANE

'It's hard to imagine now, surrounded by all this glass and concrete, but we're standing in the middle of the tinderbox that set light to London.'

We had turned off suddenly from a busy street full of cars and buses and found ourselves on what felt like a route between office buildings.

'London, at that time, was a warren of closely packed wooden houses with open flames used for cooking, heating and light. In this lane, Thomas Farriner, the king baker, had his shop and it's believed it was here, just after midnight on Sunday 2 September 1666 that a fire started.'

Aunt Bea raised her hands and started to walk quickly as she spoke.

'In high winds, it spread quickly, reaching the warehouses full of flammable cargo. Luckily there was a piece missing on London Bridge, which meant it couldn't spread south of the river. But there was plenty for it to get on with north of the river. The authorities dithered and by the time they acted it was too late and the sparks spread across the whole of London.

'It destroyed more than 13,000 houses, almost a hundred churches and one St Paul's Cathedral. It is said that it was so hot that the lead melted off the roof. London was a city of ash.

'Eventually the authorities used explosives to create firebreaks so it couldn't spread, and just under five days later it was put out. It was utterly cataclysmic, with almost a hundred thousand people left homeless.

'There had been another eruption of the bubonic plague the year before, and some have even suggested that in burning away the conditions that allowed it to flourish, the fire may have ultimately saved lives, allowing London to be rebuilt and renewed. Now, that's given me quite a thirst. Let's find somewhere to sit and have a lemonade and look at some of our puzzles.'

QUESTIONS

■ Easy

1. How many saints are named on the map?

2. What is the lowest surveyed height on the map?

■ Medium

3. How many art gallery symbols are indicated on the map?

4. The circle which has its centre in the blue crucifix marking St. Paul's Cathedral and which passes through the centre of the Tower of London, also passes through which traders' market?

■ Tricky

5. Following pink main roads, which is further from Elephant and Castle Tube station, Blackfriars Tube station or Monument Tube station?

6. With respect to the map, which of these is the odd one out: Fenchurch Street, London Bridge, Cannon Street or Blackfriars?

■ Challenging

7. Can you find three numbers on the map that add up to a total of 903?

8. Can you find locations on the map that are anagrams of the following words or phrases? Ignore the spaces and punctuation, which may differ from those in the place names.

a. BRICKS FEAR APRIL

b. DATA EAGLETS

c. ENCHANTED PATELLAS

d. THE ORCHIDS

Georgians

Map 21 BERKLEY

'For once, we're not here for the castle, my boy.'

Aunt Bea and I were looking up at a huge and excitingly brooding castle, and I had to say I was not a little disappointed.

'Twelfth century, built by Edward II, plenty of blood and intrigue and all very interesting in and of itself. But not why we're here.'

We turned around and walked down a path that took us around a pretty walled churchyard fringed with flowers. Soon we were standing in front of a sturdy white house, which Aunt Bea said was a Queen Anne-style manor house, with ivy creeping up its face.

'No, we're interested in a different Edward. Edward Jenner, a doctor who eventually saved something in the region of half a billion lives with his work.

'In the eighteenth century, smallpox, or "the speckled monster", killed 400,000 people a year in Europe and left many hundreds of thousands blinded and severely scarred. However, it was common knowledge that if you had been ill with smallpox you didn't get it again, so survivors of smallpox often nursed sufferers. It was known that you could provoke the symptoms of the disease by deliberately infecting someone with a hopefully mild version of

the disease. Indeed Jenner himself had received inoculation. But it was risky and many people died from it, plus it carried risks of spreading the pox, as patients remained infectious.

'As a country boy, Jenner had heard the stories that milkmaids who caught the much milder disease cowpox from their cows didn't get smallpox, and when a local woman came to him with cowpox, he decided to test it on a young boy. He rubbed material from the cowpox pocks into a scratch on the boy's arm. The boy became ill with cowpox a few days later but recovered, and when Jenner brought him into contact with material from smallpox pocks, he had no reaction. Jenner repeated the experiment and wrote up his findings repeatedly over the coming years. It was from this that our modern science of vaccination springs.

'From this point in time, we'll be dallying with the Georgians awhile. It's a fascinating period, which I have long been enamoured with and which I think has often suffered unfairly in comparison to what came before and after. In the meantime, I know these puzzles will be fascinating!'

QUESTIONS

Easy

1. Where would you find the digits 4 and 6 together on the map?

2. How many yellow roads are shown on the map?

Medium

3. Which survey height mark is nearest to the edge of the map?

4. How many instances on the map are there of the letters R, A and K appearing next to each other in that order?

Tricky

5. Which residential area on the map sounds the most like a starved woodland?

6. With respect to the map, which of the following is the odd one out: 15, 19, 21 or 26?

Challenging

7. If you draw a circle with its centre at the topmost corner of the woodland south of Lobthorn Covert which goes through Park House, which earthworks does it also go through?

8. Can you piece these fragments back together to make four locations shown on the map: ARK, ARM, BER, DBR, ESF, EYS, FL, FOR, GAT, IDGE, IFFP, ION, KEL, MAT, OOD, TAT, TCL, WHI?

Map 22 MAYFAIR

'It was on this street where a man named Ignatius Sancho had his shop.'

We had left Hyde Park and walked down an impressive avenue of grand, tall town houses.

'It is 1774, and trouble is brewing in the American Colonies that will lead to them declaring independence within two years. But in this year's election, Ignatius becomes the first person of African descent (whom historians know of) to vote in an election in England. He was born an enslaved person and brought to Greenwich. In spite of the protestations of the wealthy sisters who owned him that a Black child shouldn't be taught to read and write, the Duke and Duchess of Montagu, who lived nearby, provided books. Ignatius went and worked as a butler for the Duchess, and later as a valet to her son-in-law. He wrote plays, songs, and a book on musical theory, became famous as an abolitionist and corresponded at length with famous novelists urging them to condemn slavery in the British West Indies. In his forties, he opened his shop with the Montagu family's help.'

As we walked through the tree-lined streets, Aunt Bea explained that Georgian London at this time would have been full of many enslaved and free Black people.

'We must not forget that millions of enslaved people were taken from their homelands and forced to work in the colonies that produced so much wealth in Britain. We must look all of our past in the eye. Though there were a great many British people who fought for the abolition of slavery, it was a long struggle with much resistance. The slave trade was abolished in the British Empire in 1808, although slavery remained legal, but finally in 1838 the slaves were freed.

■ Easy

1. Which location name contains the most letters, ignoring punctuation?

2. How many B-road numbers are printed on the map?

■ Medium

3. What do the names John, Mary and May have in common?

4. Which full or partial grid section contains the most places of worship, starting with 1A at the top left and with numbers increasing downwards and letters increasing to the right?

■ Tricky

5. With respect to the map, which of the following is the odd one out: 31, 33, 38 and 42?

6. Which Tube station on the map lent its name to a humorous game popularised on the radio show 'I'm Sorry I Haven't A Clue?'

■ Challenging

7. From the Science Museum, head north to a music hall and then follow the main road east to the second Tube station's building. Take the next left and then third right, keep going to an A-road, and turn left to a major crossroads. Head west to another Tube station marker, then jump to the nearest blue symbol indicating a recreation centre. Turn straight north to a place of worship, and then head west to a sporting location. Where are you?

8. Can you piece these fragments back together to make four locations shown on the map: AME, ATP, DS, EET, ESE, GRE, MAD, NDS, NE, NTI, OR, ROT, ROW, RPE, SAU, TEN, TH, TLA, TR, TUS?

Map 23 STEVENTON

'It is a truth universally acknowledged, that a single man in possession of a map must tell his aunt where they must go next.'

'Very funny.'

We were looking into a field in Hampshire, while a couple of cows gazed at us with curiosity.

'I'm almost completely sure the rectory was over there,' she said, pointing towards two tall trees. 'The site of the house where the novelist Jane Austen was born and spent the first twenty-five years of her life. It is where she began drafting those famous novels. For many people, Austen, or the television adaptations at least, are what they think of when they think of British history. The dresses, the dancing, the social climbing and the romances. When I was a girl, I loved Lizzy Bennet as if she were one of my friends. Austen's heroines were intelligent, funny and knew their own minds. And yet she was forced to publish her novels anonymously, as the world of letters wasn't open to her, and saw only mild success in her own lifetime.

The obsession with marriage in her novels is a stark reminder for me of how women relied utterly on men for their social standing.'

We strolled under the shade of oak trees as insects buzzed around us and birds darted and swooped above.

'We're about three miles south of the edge of the North Wessex Downs. Utterly stunning country. We must come back here and do some proper walking one day – so much to see: Avebury, the White Horse at Uffington. But forgive me if we linger here a while longer now.

'In 2011 an archaeological dig here uncovered all sorts of household objects, which gave us a fascinating insight into their lives then. What we learned from the dig was that her life was nowhere near as grand as the world she writes about in her novels. She was writing with her nose pressed up against the window of the big house, not living within. I like to think that a woman of such quick wit would have enjoyed solving a puzzle or two along with her tea. Let's solve some in her honour.'

▦ Easy

1. How many woods, copses and plantations are named on the map?

2. Where on the map can you find the letters P, T, S and D in the same location name, but not necessarily adjacent?

▦ Medium

3. Which different types of tree are contained within words printed on the map?

4. How many separate contour lines do you cross moving directly from the letter K in Wayfarer's Walk to the letter B in Berrydown Copse?

▦ Tricky

5. Which aerial survey height point is furthest from the edge of the map?

6. With respect to the map, which of the following is the odd one out: ANGER, FOLLY, ITCH, RAGE or VENT?

▦ Challenging

7. The circle that has its centre in the church south of Steventon and which passes through the 116m ground survey height also passes through several other location names. Which is the longest?

8. Which two place names can be combined to form the anagram HENRY PROPOSES BACKWARD?

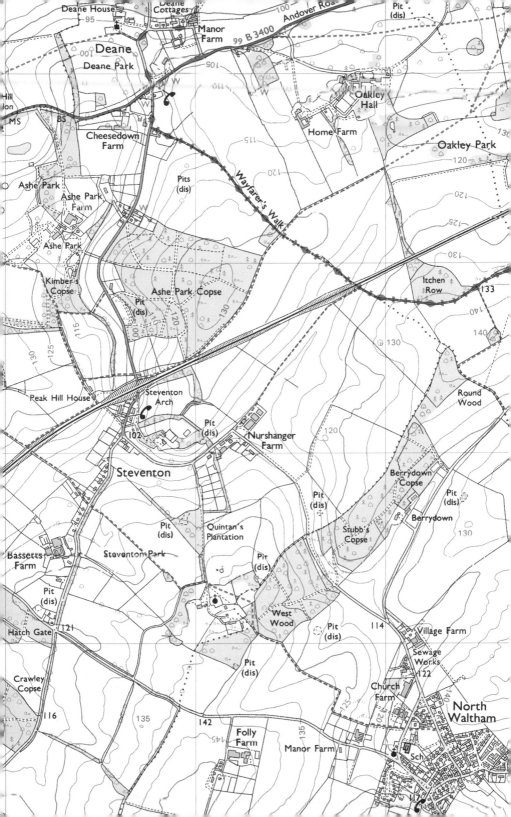

Map 24 KIRKCALDY

'There is a fine tradition of Scottish minds shaping the world, my boy.'

We were walking down from the ruins of another castle, one that Aunt Bea wanted to see if only for a moment, as it featured in a poem by Sir Walter Scott. The sea turned over white and grey to our left.

'They've found all sorts of Bronze Age sites around here. Not far from here has been claimed as the site of the Battle of Raith when King Áedán mac Gabráin of Dál Riata led an alliance of Picts, Scots and Britons against the Angles in 596, and we know that Malcolm II granted the shire of "Kircaladinit" to the church at Dunfermline in 1075. You'll find no old walls here – the sea was their main defence. And it was to become a usefully placed trading centre, able to reach the Low Countries, England, as well as the north of France.'

We stopped for a moment to admire the view and Aunt Bea explained that Kirkcaldy's nickname was 'the Lang Toun' because of the early town's long main street. As we walked the long curve of the bay facing out on to the Firth of Forth, I could well imagine it.

'There had always been a fierce intellectual tradition in Scotland and an emphasis on education. I put it down to an independent streak and perhaps even an understandable desire to separate oneself from the southern consensus.

'This became crystallised during what we now know as the Scottish Enlightenment, the period when several influential thinkers and writers reshaped our sense of how the world worked. From the philosopher David Hume to the geologist James Hutton and the poet Robert Burns, but it's another son of Kirkcaldy we're here to mainly talk about – Adam Smith.

'He was a man of prodigious gifts – a philosopher and economist, and Professor of Logic at University of Glasgow doncha know – who had travelled in Europe and met some of the leading intellectuals of the day, including Rousseau and Voltaire.

'With his book, *The Wealth of Nations*, he wrote the first major work of political economy, which made the case for free trade. In a country and world that was in the process of being transformed by technology, industry and commerce, his ideas would be enormously influential. I like to imagine him pacing up and down the long streets here. Now, open that bag and fetch me a wealth of puzzles.'

■ Easy

1. How many post offices are shown on the map?

2. Which location name on the map is the longest?

■ Medium

3. If you subtract the highest surveyed height shown on the map from the largest road number, what is the result?

4. With respect to the map, which of the following is the odd one out: Linktown, Port Brae, Pathhead, Sinclairtown or West Gallatown?

■ Tricky

5. How many blue symbols on the map indicate opportunities for physical exercise?

6. What is the minimum number of educational institutions listed on the map?

■ Challenging

7. Can you find locations on the map that are anagrams of the following words or phrases? Ignore the spaces and punctuation, which may differ from those in the place names.

    a. CANDID SKYLARKS

    b. TWIN CLARIONS

    c. HARD OLD APRON

    d. NEED GARLIC

8. From the first letter of a home for pigeons, head precisely west to a place of worship. Come out on to the road and turn left then right and then second left, and follow the road to a B-road. There is an adjacent blue symbol; go to the building it refers to, and move a short way west to a clearly marked route. Follow that route north until it intersects a B-road. Which named historic feature is to the north-west?

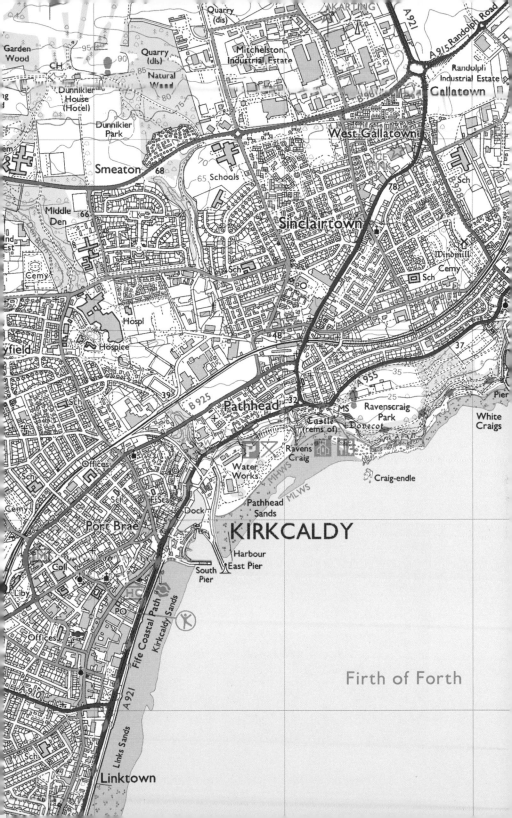

Map 25 SHREWSBURY

'Because we're having a hard enough time fitting in so much human history, I haven't made many diversions into these islands' pre-human history.'

We were crossing the River Severn across a thin bridge on our way through the pleasingly jumbled buildings of Shrewsbury. Aunt Bea explained how at one time Shrewsbury had been the capital of the Kingdom of Powys on the other side of Offa's Dyke and was settled throughout the medieval period, being a key location in the wool industry in the fourteenth and fifteenth centuries. We walked past a great many original timber-framed houses from the fifteenth and sixteenth centuries.

'The planet was teeming with life for hundreds of millions of years before anything approaching our ancestors took their first steps. Through the long lens of geological time, humans are a very recent inconvenience. A blink of an eye in the 3.5 billion-year-old story of life on earth. It was to be the remains of some of that life that were so key in transforming our understanding of the world around us.'

It was a famous son of Shrewsbury who was to transform our understanding of how life came to exist.

'Charles Darwin was born in The Mount, which we shall arrive at in about five minutes. He is, of course, famous for his theory of evolution by natural selection in *On the Origin of Species*. It was an idea that caused outrage among many, challenging the biblical account of creation. From observing many different sorts of animals all around the world, but especially species on the Galapagos Islands, he was able to put together his theory that within species there could be variation and that if that variation made the organism more likely to survive and breed successfully, they would be passed on to the next generation – the idea that gets shortened to "survival of the fittest" and which, by the way, has nothing to go with gym membership.'

I made a face and as we strolled said it was interesting to be in a town where the buildings seemed to pass through various time periods, as if they were at different stages of architectural evolution. But when I said that to Aunt Bea, she just harrumphed.

'Why don't you do some adapting to your environment and find me some of those puzzles.'

Easy

1. How many times does the word 'HILL' appear on the map?

2. Which place of worship is closest to the edge of the map?

Medium

3. Which road number shown on the map includes the digits 4, 6 and 8?

4. How many location names on the map contain words associated with nobility?

Tricky

5. With respect to the map, which of the following is the odd one out: 19, 38, 45, 51 and 72?

6. Where on the map would you find a circle quartered by a cross?

Challenging

7. What is the least number of turns required to travel by road from the hospital to the school at Greenfields?

8. Which two place names can be combined to form the anagram FOUND TALKING MINDLESS?

Victorians

Map 26 LOUGHBOROUGH

'Here would be a fine place for us to pick up our regular argument over your obsession with screen machines, my boy.'

I made a face, always dreading that particular subject coming up. We were standing in front of a town hall, which Aunt Bea informed me was a marvellous example of the mid-nineteenth-century Italianate style, and which I had to admit definitely looked like it had been dropped into place from a different country.

'This neck of the woods will always be linked to a tension where disruptive technologies are concerned. It was in these parts that one of the final destructive acts said to have been carried out in the name of the Luddites took place. The Luddites were a secret group of textile workers who reacted to the ongoing mechanisation of their industry by destroying factory machinery. They were named after the almost certainly fictitious Ned Ludd. What was true, however, was the systematic destruction of machinery by those who lost their jobs due to mechanisation. Though there were stories

of disgruntled workers breaking their equipment from earlier, it lasted officially from 1811 to 1816. There are some who doubt that the attack on a lace-making factory here was even connected to the Luddites, but rather believe it was a rival factory owner's attempts at sabotage.

'Luddite or not, the attack on John Heathcoat's bobbinet machines was the last major event in a long series of destructive acts against industrial machinery. The Luddites are a reminder that what looks to us at a distance like the long, clean natural arc of progress, with a logic to each age succeeding another, was nothing like as neat to live through. When we trace our fingers over a map, when we pass over warehouses and factories, old industrial districts and docks, when we stand in the place where history happened, we remember that these were people whose lives were transformed, not always happily.'

Aunt Bea lamented the fact that we wouldn't have time to reach the Peak District on this trip, but promised me we would have time to see the steam engines at the Great Central Railway.

'Now if it isn't too ironic, perhaps you could get out one of your devices and find us a café. We can sit and you can help this old Luddite solve some of our puzzles.'

■ Easy

1. How many public telephones are shown on the map?

2. In total, how many wells and springs are marked on the map?

■ Medium

3. Which column of the map grid contains the fewest schools?

4. Where on the map will you find a pub near some schools?

■ Tricky

5. Which location's name contains a word that is one letter change away from being a place to moor a ship?

6. How many locations printed on the map contain words that are types of drink within their letters?

■ Challenging

7. Using only the initial letters of words that appear on the map in blue, can you find a 5-letter word describing a solid shape?

8. The following block of simple cipher text identifies four locations on the map.

   Can you identify them?
   OOTKHRE
   FSLRTAR
   NNEALET
   AOBPEPN
   TDRNHRE
   SRAOSOC

Map 27 SHILDON

'It is such a part of our view of this era – the plume of smoke from a steam train making its way through the green of the countryside. That "chuff chuff chuff, woo woo", immediately transporting us to somewhere else.'

Aunt Bea and I were standing on an unassuming dusty brick bridge over a railway. Beneath us the silver- and rust-coloured rails ran.

'There is an argument that of all the technology that transformed our world, perhaps the most transformative of all was the steam engine. In factories, on boats and in mines, it supercharged everything it touched. But it was to be in the transport of humans and goods across land that it was truly revolutionary. Richard Trevithick had taken his friends for a ride on his "Puffing Devil" in 1801 and Matthew Murray built his Salamanca in 1812, but in 1825, for the first time, thousands of spectators watched George Stevenson's Locomotion No. 1 steam locomotive haul a train of passengers on a public railway.'

She pointed down at the tracks, as if she could see it.

'They say there were a thousand passengers in sixty wagons and thousands came to cheer this miracle.

'The railways would transform this island and the world, collapsing the distances that people could travel. Before the railways it took four days to travel from London to Manchester. Within decades of what happened here, it took four hours. There was an economic explosion and an acceleration of the move away from farming to factories and villages to towns and cities. In 1750, only 15 per cent of the population lived in towns, but by 1900 it was 85 per cent. It is steam that takes us puffing triumphantly into the Victorian era.'

Aunt Bea took a step back, her eyes glinting.

'We are in the middle of an astonishing coalescence of natural beauty here, with the North York Moors forty miles to the south-east of us, the North Pennines Area of Outstanding Natural Beauty thirty miles to our west and the Yorkshire Dales thirty miles to our south-west. We even have the Lake District less than sixty miles away.'

She hitched her bag up higher on to her shoulders.

'Railways are such a familiar element to any map, but every time I run my finger over one, I am filled with a sense of their thrilling adventure. Speaking of adventure, let us find some puzzles to occupy ourselves with.'

Easy

1. Where is the largest continuous patch of woodland on the map?

2. How many complete orange contour line heights are shown on the bottom row of the map grid?

Medium

3. Are there more public telephones or museums shown on the map?

4. What is the elevation of the lowest surveyed height on the map?

Tricky

5. Where can you find the letters ILL near the letters IDD?

6. Can you find three numbers on the map that sum to seven less than 500?

Challenging

7. Which words printed on the map contain within them a word that is a type of vehicle?

8. How many unique examples are there of complete words on the map that are also common adjectives (e.g. 'Short', 'Full', 'White', etc.)?

Map 28 FARNE ISLANDS

'I want you to imagine, my boy, that you are a passenger on a steamship, travelling north through storm and fog from Hull to Dundee.'

The fact that we were sitting looking out over a calm sea made it tricky, but I screwed my eyes up and tried especially hard.

'In the midst of the boiling sea, the engines fail and the ship is dashed against the rocks. Many passengers drown, but nine people make it to the lifeboat and another nine somehow clamber on to the rocks. As dawn breaks, Grace Darling, the 22-year-old daughter of a lighthouse keeper spots the wreck and she and her father launch the North Sunderland lifeboat. Conditions are treacherous and they row against vicious winds and tides past jagged rocks until they reach the survivors. Her father leaps on to the rocks and she is left to keep the boat safe and steady on her own. When she and her father had finished, they had rescued all nine of the survivors. The story caused a global news sensation, with Grace heralded by some as the bravest woman ever.'

Aunt Bea raised her eyebrow.

'What is certainly true is that she was the first woman ever to receive a Royal National Lifeboat Institution medal and even got fifty quid from Queen Victoria. I love this story for many reasons. Partly because it reminds us that even in the middle of so much industrial power, so much expansive

confidence, we were still an island, still governed by the sea and cowed by nature. Partly because of the story of her bravery and the huge outcry, I choose to focus on the incredulity that a woman could be brave and it says more about those in control of the media than women's capability for heroic behaviour. I reckon that for every one story noticed, there are a thousand invisible Graces whose deeds went unreported.'

We were walking through the pretty stone harbour at Seahouses with fishing boats when Aunt Bea continued.

'The islands they were wrecked upon – the Farne Islands – are a miraculous place for wildlife. Those cliffs are stained white by the droppings of seabirds. There are more than twenty species of seabirds, with an enormous colony of puffins and a brilliant place to spot grey seal pups. If we have got our timings right, I'd like to try for one of the voyages to the islands.'

'You could say, in many ways, she was very much a media darling,' I said.

'I am going to pretend I didn't hear that,' said Aunt Bea. 'Now fetch some puzzles quickly.'

■ Easy

1. How many times does the word 'Gut' appear on the map?

2. What is the highest point shown on the map?

■ Medium

3. Which location name sounds a little like unexpected guests?

4. Which word on the map is one letter change from being a famous Egyptian pharaoh?

■ Tricky

5. Which location on the map shares a name with a major port in north-east England?

6. How many fully separate islands and rocks are shown on the map, not counting islands fully or partially duplicated within the excerpted region to the bottom right of the map?

■ Challenging

7. There are six numbers printed in the excerpted region shown towards the bottom right of the map. Using each of these six numbers exactly once, performing only the elemental mathematical operations – addition, subtraction, multiplication and division – can you arrive at a total of exactly 350?

8. Which two place names can be combined to form the anagram ANOTHER UNDERWEIGHT PERSON?

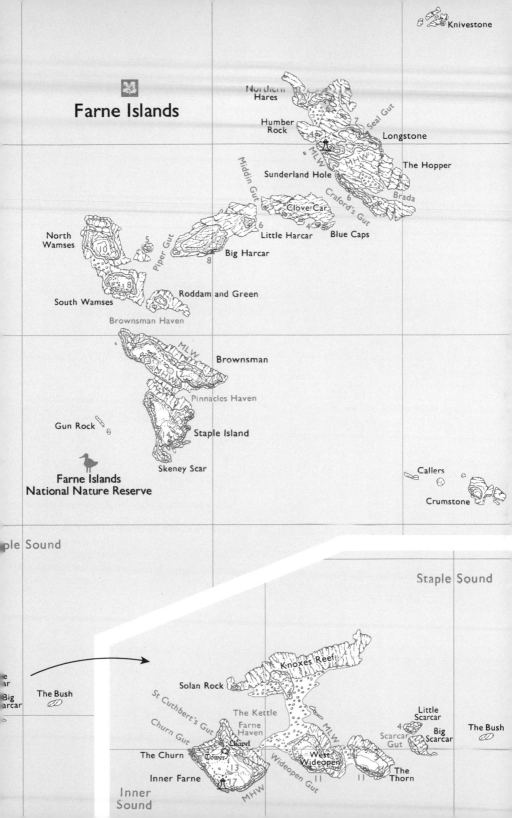

Farne Islands

Knivestone

Northern Hares

Humber Rock

Seal Gut

7

Longstone

The Hopper

Sunderland Hole

Middin Gut

MLW

MHW

Craford's Gut

6

Brada

Clove Car

Blue Caps

4

North Wamses

5

Piper Gut

Little Harcar

6

Big Harcar

8

Roddam and Green

South Wamses

Brownsman Haven

MLW

MHW

Brownsman

Pinnacles Haven

Gun Rock

Staple Island

Skeney Scar

Callers

Crumstone

**Farne Islands
National Nature Reserve**

ple Sound

Staple Sound

Knoxes Reef

Solan Rock

The Bush

e
ar

Big
arcar

St Cuthbert's Gut

The Kettle

Farne
Haven

MLW

Little
Scarcar

4

Scarcar
Gut

Big
Scarcar

The Bush

Churn Gut

Chapel

The Churn

Tower

13

West
Wideopen

Wideopen Gut

Inner Farne

17

11

11

The Thorn

MHW

Inner
Sound

Map 29 NEWCASTLE UPON TYNE

'That is one of my favourite bridges anywhere,' said Aunt Bea.

We were looking at the Tyne Bridge, soaring in between Newcastle and Gateshead.

'There's just something so pleasing about that perfect parabola, the thickness of each line outlined against the sky. There are bigger and longer bridges, but this one is . . . well it's just very pleasing.'

We were walking briskly, as Aunt Bea said we had a journey of about a mile and a half in front of us.

'There are many reasons we could have visited Newcastle. It was a fort on Hadrian's Wall. William the Conqueror's son stopped off on his way back from a battle in Scotland and built a wooden castle at the main crossing point to the river, which they called "Novum Castellum" or New Castle. You can still see some of the twenty-five-foot thick walls from the Middle Ages, and it supported Charles I during the Civil War. It was a key part of the Industrial Revolution; a workshop that built great steel ships and steam trains.'

Eventually she took a pause for breath.

'However, I want to take you to the house on Summerhill Grove where a woman called Anna Richardson and her sister-in-law Ellen lived. It was here in 1846 that they had the abolitionist, writer and former slave

Frederick Douglass to stay with them.'

Aunt Bea explained that he was on a lecture tour around Britain and Ireland, where he was telling his story. Douglass had published his autobiography the previous year, *Narrative of the Life of Frederick Douglass, an American Slave* and he was travelling across Great Britain and Ireland on a lecture tour.

'Though by this time slavery was abolished in the British Empire, it was still legal in the USA and Douglass was still enslaved. Anna and Ellen raised the money and instructed a US lawyer to buy his freedom. By the following year he wrote to them to say that he held his papers of freedom in his hand.'

We stood and looked up at the row of neat, unassuming houses.

'As well as the great battles, the palaces, the monuments and landmarks, there is history of this sort, hidden history, often perhaps unknown by people two streets away. But it is no less remarkable. The land around us all is rich with all sorts of hidden treasures. The name of a landmark on a map can be the key to unlocking an untold mystery. The past is a puzzle waiting to be solved. Speaking of which . . .'

QUESTIONS

■ Easy

1. How many times does the word 'Moor' appear on the map?

2. Where on the map can you find the letters DAL near the letters SIN?

■ Medium

3. What is the greatest surveyed height shown on the map?

4. How many unique examples are there of complete words on the map which are also possessive nouns (i.e. 'Bill's', 'Janet's', 'Jones'', etc.)?

■ Tricky

5. How many sporting and exercise-related locations are shown on the map?

6. Can you find three different numbers on the map that add up to twenty less than 1,000?

■ Challenging

7. From a museum near a cathedral, head directly north to the first main road. Find the most easterly point of that road on the map, and head westwards. Take the first right, and follow the road to a junction flanked by places of worship. Head directly north to a pair of places of worship with spires, minarets or domes. Take the road heading west from that piece of land, and follow it to a piece of parkland. There is a body of water in a south-westerly direction. Where is it?

8. Using only the capital letters of the printed names of bridges crossing the River Tyne, can you find a seven-letter word for 'drinks'?

Map 30 KENNINGTON

'I didn't take you for a big cricket fan, Aunt Bea,' I said, as we squinted up at the London Oval in the sunshine.

'Oh, I have certainly known the joy of the thwack of willow upon leather, my boy. In my opinion there aren't many games that can't be improved by the addition of lunch and tea. However, we are here for a far less obviously visible reason.'

We walked through alongside a quiet brick estate.

'This area was incorporated into London in 1855, but it was recorded in the Domesday Book as Chenintune, and for much of its life it was effectively a village on the southern roads into London. A certain Geoffrey Chaucer was employed as Clerk of the Works.

'Royal Surrey Gardens is no longer here, but it was there in July 1857 that a four-day military festival was held to raise funds for Mary Seacole. Mary had been born in Jamaica and when the Crimean War broke out, she came to volunteer as a nurse here in England. But she was repeatedly told that "no more nurses were needed" though she knew it was because of her colour. So she travelled to Crimea and set up her own hospital. There she earned the

nickname "Mother Seacole" and won acclaim for treating soldiers of both sides who had been injured in battle.

'When she returned to Britain, she had very little money and support from the government, but soldiers wrote letters to newspapers telling the stories of what she had done and they organised the fundraising event, which was attended by thousands of people and later her autobiography became a bestseller.

'So many layers of history, overlapping each other. Where we are walking is thought to have been a sacred place of assembly in prehistoric times. There are stories like this waiting just under the surface, every time you run your finger over a map. Now, as it feels only appropriate, what say we break for lunch and some puzzles?'

Easy

1. What is the largest train station shown on the map?

2. Which is the furthest from the Imperial War Museum, the Oval or the London Eye?

Medium

3. Which full or partial grid row contains the most locations identified as schools, colleges and/or academies, counting plurals as two schools and assigning each location to the grid row that its written label appears in?

4. Which pink circle with a horizontal bar through it (representing the presence of a Tube station) is nearest to the edge of the map?

Tricky

5. Which bridge shares a name with a British car manufacturer?

6. What do CROSS, HALL, HOUSE and TOWER have in common?

Challenging

7. Staying exclusively on A-roads and B-roads, what is the least number of turns required to travel from the south-west corner of Buckingham Palace to Somerset House without leaving the map?

8. Can you find locations on the map that are anagrams of the following words or phrases? Ignore the spaces and punctuation, which may differ from those in the place names.
   a. CAPABLE HAMLET
   b. SECRET EQUALISER
   c. SMARTER HIVE
   d. ARSENAL TOUCHES

Map 31 MANCHESTER

'We could have visited Manchester for any number of reasons. The magnificent Pennines lying to the north of us are two to three million years old. We could have visited when it was a stronghold of the Brigantes tribe, or when it was Mamucium in Roman times, or during any of the eras in which it was continuously settled after that. We could have visited in the height of the Industrial Revolution. But the reason I've chosen to visit today is because of a woman called Emmeline Pankhurst, who was born in Moss Side in 1858.'

We were walking south past Deansgate locks on the Rochdale Canal with its red brick viaduct, and Aunt Bea was out ahead of me as usual, calling back all the time.

'Emmeline was born into a wealthy and politically active family and would go on to be a driving force in the fight for women's right to vote. She grew up in a time when women did not have the right to vote in elections, and Queen Victoria famously called the battle for women's rights a "mad, wicked folly". However, all through the mid nineteenth century there had been pressure building for women to be extended the same voting rights as men. Emmeline was part of a movement known as the suffragists, which campaigned for votes for women.

'But in 1903, likely frustrated by the suffragists' non-confrontational approach to campaigning, she formed an organisation called the Women's Social and Political Union, whose members were the first to be christened "suffragettes". They were involved in fierce protests that involved demonstrations, arson and window smashing. Their motto was "deeds not words" and over the coming years, many were arrested and went on hunger strike, but were force-fed.

'The first group of women were granted the right to vote in 1918 (women over the age of thirty who owned property or had a university degree), with all women over the age of twenty-one following in 1928. Emmeline's life work played a critical role in achieving this result, and she died in London in the same year at the age of sixty-nine.

'Now let's take a look at some puzzles...'

Easy

1. How many times does the word 'Park' appear on the map?

2. Which is the most elevated place of worship on the map?

Medium

3. Where on the map can you find the word TWO? The 'two' letters are adjacent and in that order.

4. What do the words GATE, LOCK, MOTE and RING all have in common on the map?

Tricky

5. Which three different road numbers add up to a total of 17,767?

6. Which location's name contains a word that is one letter change away from being a type of dishware?

Challenging

7. Using five separate survey points on the map, how can you arrive at 2,999 using addition, subtraction, multiplication and division?

8. The following block of simple cipher text identifies four locations on the map. Can you identify them?
   AAQUC ISTCE NERTA
   DENSA EGTAS TINOT
   CEHEH IRSGI
   NRCHO RADEL ACALN

Map 32 TREDEGAR

'Our route has often seemed almost linear but sometimes it has strange echoes and loops, my boy.'

We were looking over a low metal fence at a series of jumbled, spaced-out gravestones.

'These hills are rich with history. There is evidence of Bronze and Iron Age settlements all around here. But what we are looking at now is the Cefn Golau Cholera Cemetery. These are the graves of the local people who died in two cholera epidemics in 1832 and 1849.'

It was an incredible place to think about the past, with the narrow ridge of the mountains, the different greens and the shadow of the clouds moving across the hillside.

'We see the symbol for a hospital on a map and we don't think it is remarkable. But of course our modern conception of healthcare is so recent. Here in 1897, a boy called Aneurin Bevan was born to a coalmining family in the last years of Victoria's reign. He was to go on and found the NHS, which flourished in the spirit of social reform after the Second World War. But prior to the government taking control of the health service and nationalising

it – as it was for much of the history of these islands – the sort of healthcare you received was down to your ability to pay for it. Those too poor to afford doctors relied on infirmaries at workhouses or voluntary hospitals, which were funded by the wealthy to take care of the poor. There was still the long shadow of the Poor Law and those Victorian workhouses, which would supply rudimentary healthcare, food and clothing in exchange for manual labour, though conditions there meant they certainly weren't top of anyone's list of places to visit.

'Bevan had grown up seeing the benefits of the Tredegar Medical Aid Society, which provided healthcare to all its members in return for a very small weekly blanket fee. This gave him the model for the National Health Service, and despite fierce opposition from both Labour and Conservative politicians – and the British Medical Association – the NHS came into being in 1946. He tried to do the same for social housing, with less success, and was shortly afterwards forced out of government by his party leadership.

'Without Aneurin Bevan's ferocious sense of what was right, the country would be a much poorer, weaker thing now. He is truly one of the great Welsh heroes. His legacy shields us still, and it is more important than ever in these uncertain times.'

Easy

1. How many instances of the Welsh word 'y', meaning 'the', appear on the map?

2. Where on the map would you find a cemetery next to a rubbish tip?

 Medium

3. How many pubs are shown on the map?

4. Where can you find the letters ANT near to the letters WAY?

Tricky

5. Which is further from the public telephone, the bus station at Tredegar or the aerial survey point on Rhymney Hill?

6. With respect to the map, which of the following is the odd one out: 346, 356, 366 or 376?

Challenging

7. Can you piece these fragments back together to make four locations shown on the map: ACH, AFO, EF, FRE, GA, HIR, NF, NSI, NSI, RFA, RH, SCW, SIO, YWI?

8. Which two place names can be combined to form the anagram HORSEWHIPS FOR DELIVERY?

Twentieth
Century

Map 33 SCARBOROUGH

As we walked up a steep, winding path towards ruins, Aunt Bea was as serious as I'd ever seen her.

'It is virtually impossible to overstate the importance of the First World War and its impact all across Britain. There are tens of thousands of war memorials from this period spread across the land, and one's thoughts turn to the Cenotaph in London and the National Memorial Arboretum in Staffordshire, but every village in England lost loved ones in those foreign fields. The Great War is a subject one could spend several lifetimes exploring.

'But I wanted to bring you here because at 8 a.m. on Wednesday 16 December, roughly 500 shells rained down from the two German battleships that appeared. People, completely understandably, thought that this was the beginning of a German invasion of Britain. Remember, this was a war that many people thought would be over by Christmas. One of their first targets was Scarborough Castle. It feels like a remarkable collapsing of history to me that a castle, which had been here since midway through the twelfth century, and had been a key fortress throughout the medieval period and seen heavy damage during the Civil War, was to have its walls breached by twentieth-century warfare.

'There was heavy damage in Hartlepool and Whitby too, but the attack on civilians in Scarborough scandalised the world at the time. An important reminder I think that these events are, in the long history of these islands, really only the blink of an eye. The twelfth and twentieth centuries may seem far apart to us, and 1914 may appear unimaginably

long ago to you, but we can find traces of it all around us. We can explore the land, and we can walk the roads the postman was walking on his rounds that morning when the shells began to fall. Wherever we are we do not have to travel far to be walking directly in the footsteps of history.'

As we walked back down from the castle and I saw the curve of the bay and the houses nestled against the hillside, I imagined what it must have been like to wake up that morning as a child, probably looking forward to Christmas. We were both thoughtful as we made our way back into town, doing some puzzles along the way.

■ Easy

1. Which road number is nearest to the edge of the map?

2. What is the elevation of the contour line that encloses the circular clearing at the north end of Oliver's Mount?

■ Medium

3. How many locations on the map contain words that are also common men's first names – other than Cliff?

4. Are there more sporting facilities or miscellaneous tourist sites (indicated by a blue star) shown on the map?

■ Tricky

5. Where might you find some abandoned curds and whey?

6. The circle that has its centre in the dome at the top of the lighthouse symbol in the harbour and passes through the 61m aerial survey height south of Holbeck Gardens also passes through the central portion of which word?

■ Challenging

7. Which three surveyed heights shown on the map can be added together to reach a total of 100?

8. With respect to the map, what do the words CAR, DEN and EAT have in common?

Betty Muffet Rocks

Northstead
Manor
Gardens

27

North Bay

Northstead

Coffee Pot

Remains of
Chapel of Our Lady
on remains of
ROMAN
SIGNAL
STATION

FB

FBs

Heasholm
Park

Lake

The
Holms

Castle
Cliff

North Sands

9

Castle
(rems of)

78

FBs

Cricket
Gd

Clarence
Gardens

Hall
(rems of)

Cemetery

F.Sta

Gambol Stones

A165

Sch

Old
Harbour

Luna Park
Fun Fair

IRB &
LB Sta

dlands

A64

MHW

B1363

Lib'y
St Nicholas
Cliff

East
Harbour

Schs

England Coast Path

Cliff Lift

Superstore

Coll

A64

South Sands

SCARBOROUGH

Mean Low Water

South Cliff

The Spa Complex

Falsgrave

Cliff Lift

grave
ark

South
Cliff
Gardens

South Bay

sr

Weaponness

South
Cliff

Star Disk

Univ

Holbeck
Gardens

War
Mem'l
Resrs

61

Slipway

FB

155

School

B1427

van

82

Wheatcroft Cliff

Black
Rocks

College

94

Cleveland Way

ehill

94

University

Schs

Wheatcroft

135

CH

Oliver's Mount Plantation

135

A165

69

Oliver's Mount

130

Scarborough
South Cliff
Golf Club

A641

The
Mere

125

Knox
Hill

FBs

116

Map 34 JARROW

'One of the reasons I am so keen for us to get out and about and walk, my boy, is because it connects us so directly to the vast majority of human history. Yes, humans have augmented their ability to move around with horses and then with various ingenious devices. But we are bipeds, standing on our two legs, and for much of human history we have walked to get about the place. Walking is the rhythm of human history from those first footsteps preserved in the mudflats.'

We were walking along the south bank of the Tyne.

'And so it was when a group of 200 protesters, led by their redoubtable MP, a woman called Ellen Wilkinson, wanted to draw attention to the mass unemployment and poverty in the north-east of England and specifically the town of Jarrow. They marched almost 300 miles to London, to deliver a petition to the prime minister, Stanley Baldwin.

'Britain was in the middle of a global depression, following on from the Great Depression, which had begun in the United States and had spread throughout the world. It hit industrial and mining areas hardest, devastating many places in Wales and Scotland. In Jarrow, which was reliant on the employment of one large shipyard, it was utterly devastating when it closed.

'North across the Tyne, we are a stone's throw from Wallsend, the furthest east that Hadrian's

Wall reached. We have the Jarrow Crusaders' route over the next four weeks as they travelled south. They were met sometimes with indifference and sometimes celebration. There is debate as to how much was directly changed by the march – reportedly the petition disappeared sharpish and is yet to be found – but the public sympathy it won changed a lot of attitudes, and the story of those citizens marching down to the powers that be has always fascinated me. Think of it, as we trace their route on a map, the different eras of history we travel through moving from the north to the south, the old territories, old kingdoms, forgotten boundaries. An area that utterly relied on an industry that now feels like a relic of history. We live as if our age is normal and will endure. But all it takes to turn us into history is time. We do well to keep that in mind when we go on an adventure with a map.'

■ Easy

1. What is the lowest survey height shown on the map?

2. Where would you find nine circles in close proximity?

■ Medium

3. Which location name contains the most letters, ignoring punctuation?

4. Moving directly from the place of worship nearest to the edge of the map to the symbol marking the Leisure Pool, how many coloured roads do you pass through?

■ Tricky

5. Going by number labels printed on the map, how many different A and B roads are indicated?

6. Which location's name contains a word that is one letter change away from being a milk drink?

■ Challenging

7. What do you get if you add the number of recreation centres to the number of specified oil or gas facilities, and multiply the result by the number of the lowest-numbered A-road?

8. Can you find locations on the map that are anagrams of the following words or phrases? Ignore the spaces and punctuation, which may differ from those in the place names.
   a. RECENTLY MARTIAN
   b. TRIVIAL RE-ENTRY
   c. EDIFYING PALL
   d. STORMY FREEMASON

Map 35 WATERFOOT

'This quiet field in Waterfoot may seem like an odd place to talk about the Second World War, but it's an astonishing story and reminds us of the hidden by ways of history that surround us.

'There's evidence of Iron Age settlements in these parts and the Romans made it this far, of course. They had a settlement called Vanduara where what is now called Paisley. These fields were part of the Kingdom of Strathclyde then the Kingdom of Alba, which would become the Kingdom of Scotland.'

Aunt Bea was twisting grass together into a rope.

'It was 10 May 1941, when a German airman parachuted out of his aeroplane before it crashed. A local farmer, reportedly pitchfork in hand, arrested him and detained him back at his house before raising the alarm. He identified himself as Captain Alfred Horn and asked to pass on an important message to the Duke of Hamilton, who lived about twelve miles away. When the duke arrived, presumably already puzzled, the airman revealed himself to be Rudolf Hess, the deputy Führer of the Third Reich and one of the most senior figures in the Nazi Party, and explained that he was there to broker a peace deal between Germany and Britain.

'We must, of course, not lose sight of the tremendous impact that the events of the Second World War had across the entire country. The bombings destroyed so many areas of Britain, including Edinburgh, Aberdeen, Glasgow, Liverpool, Sheffield and Manchester. There was also the astonishing impact of evacuation on more than two million children who were sent to live away from their families. It was, as well as being incredibly hard to comprehend, a psychological process for the families involved, an astonishing and unparalleled process of revealing entirely different places and ways of life. For many children from urban areas, it was the first time they had seen the countryside.

'Hess's plan to bring peace and carve the globe into British and German Empires failed – neither Churchill nor Hitler were ever interested, and the man he came to speak to, the Duke of Hamilton, was not the influential anti-war sympathizer that Hess and his advisors had believed. Hess had hoped that King George VI would be persuaded to force the government into offering a partnership Hitler would accept. It would be a very different world now if he had somehow succeeded. Sometimes, the balance of history tilts on a knife-edge, which is something to think about... just like those puzzles of yours.'

▪ Easy

1. How many waterfalls are shown on the map?
2. Does the map show more places of worship or locations with Borland in their name?

▪ Medium

3. Where on the map would you find the letters HIT near the letters ATE?
4. With respect to the map, what do the following words have in common: BORLAND, CASTLE, DRIPPS and FLOORS?

▪ Tricky

5. How many unique examples are there on the map of words or word fragments that are also residences?
6. Without leaving the map, what is the least number of turns required to travel by road from the building at Bonnyton to the school next to the Tower?

▪ Challenging

7. Starting at the symbol for a golf club, move south to a road shown on the map in orange, and follow the contour line that passes through the first letter of its name to another instance of the same letter. There is an air survey height nearby. Jump from that to a ground survey of the same height. Follow the road north, and take the first left. When you encounter a patch of woodland to the immediate south, head north to a named body of water. Where are you?
8. Which two place names can be combined to form the anagram DEBATED WORSHIPPING FOODS?

Map 36 TYNEHAM

'So far, when we have been travelling in time, we have been forced to use our imagination, to scrape away the modern layers of what we see and travel back in time. But here is a place remarkably frozen in time.'

We were walking past an old-fashioned telephone box towards a collection of stone ruins. A shock of red flowers grew up through the stone.

'In 1943, at the height of the war, the army needed somewhere to train with tanks in preparation for the D-Day landings in France. So they requisitioned this village along with 7,500 acres of land. It was supposed to be temporary, of course. The villagers left a note on the church door for the soldiers: "Please treat the church and houses with care; we have given up our homes where many of us have lived for generations to help win the war and to keep men free. We shall return one day and thank you for treating the village kindly."

'The army never gave it back though, and instead issued a compulsory purchase order five years later. It's been in use as a range and training ground ever since. You'll see shell damage on many of the buildings – although not the ones being preserved as museums. It was a working village before the army came, with a population of 225, and most of its people were involved in farming or fishing. It had a post office, a school and a church. Signs of settlement here go back to pre-Roman times, but the Romans lived in the area as well. When the Domesday Book was compiled, the place was owned by William the Conqueror's half-brother. There's something poetic there, I suppose.

'The army's possession of the area has prevented any farming, residential development or forestry, so it's a refuge for British wildlife of all sorts. It's generally soldier-free and safe to visit at weekends and during the month of August, and as well as the

period museums' – she gestured ahead at the school building – 'there are some remarkably beautiful coastal walks that we'll make a start on a little later.'

We walked through to the school, which, like the church, had been restored as if it was still 1943. Looking around, it was easy to believe that the students had only just stepped away from their lessons, leaving books opened on the desks and chalk still on the blackboard.

'It reminds me of Pompeii. A moment of history, captured out of time. Hopefully we can preserve it down through the centuries.'

■ Easy

1. Which two survey heights are 155m apart in elevation?

2. How many different common colour names are shown on the map?

■ Medium

3. Which English word appears the most times on the map?

4. Where on the map can you find a place that sounds like a warning about investments?

■ Tricky

5. Where on the map would you find the letters APE near the letters LIST?

6. How many locations on the map include a compass direction in their name?

■ Challenging

7. Can you rearrange seven of the initial letters appearing on the map in red to find a word for an attendant at a hotel?

8. The following block of simple cipher text identifies several locations on the map. Can you identify them?

1615220914072015140809212

021201031102011818152 3

2025140508011308152 11905

2315180 2011818152320152120

Map 37 WATFORD GAP

I wasn't able to hide my impression that Watford Gap was a long way from being the most picturesque location Aunt Bea and I had ever visited together. We were standing on the footbridge between the northbound and southbound M1 services, looking down at the stream of traffic rushing in both directions.

'It may not be classically beautiful right here, my boy, but this has been the gateway between the south and the north since at least the Romans, and I like to think that Hadrian and his successors would have appreciated the functional grandeur of the motorways. Yes, there have been places with more romantic associations on our trip, but there is a pleasing symmetry and a real-world example of how the Romans and those earlier routes can be found lurking under the modern routes on a map. Each successive generation has been working with the same basic geological toolkit. We all have to live on and with the land, to shape ourselves to its reality. Because of it, within a space of less than half a kilometre, we find modern roads, railways and canals all in parallel, all following the ghost of the Roman routes. When we look at a map, there are so many aspects to it. The place names, rivers, roads, the different eras of building.

'The older ghostly markers of kingdom and tribe, those old geological bones underneath, the types of rock and soil, the great seams that run underneath, the mountains, rivers and valleys that have shaped history.

'Today, we spend so much time in an environment that we have mastery of, that we find it easy to forget the realities of geography. Cities are bubbles in their own way, and its easy to imagine that they nestle outside of the world's physical presence. But it only takes a moment to be reminded of the geology beneath us. So many of us in cities move around regularly. We move through a county barrier on a motorway, or slip across a river without really registering it. We work or go to school in one place and live in another, we travel the country. Every time we change our immediate location, we're following the literal lay of the land.

'For so much of human history of course, there was a different sort of urgency to where we were – which way a river flowed, what the boundaries were of a field, or a village, or a kingdom. There was no hiding from the reality of the ground beneath us back then. To be out and about with a map is to bring together these two sorts of understanding of where we are and who we are, informed by the confluence of landscape and history. Our motorways embody this. And if that doesn't set your mind whirring, how about a puzzle or two?'

QUESTIONS

■ Easy

1. Which motorway runs up the map?
2. What is the name of the circular patch of woodland?

■ Medium

3. Which single-font location name contains the most letters, ignoring punctuation?
4. What is the highest point identified on the map?

■ Tricky

5. Where on the map can you find the word AIR?
6. With respect to the map, what do the following words have in common: LONG, LODGE and ROMAN?

■ Challenging

7. Which four surveyed heights shown on the map can be added together to reach a total of 500?
8. Which two place names can be combined to form the anagram DOWNHILL GEOGRAPHY TITLE?

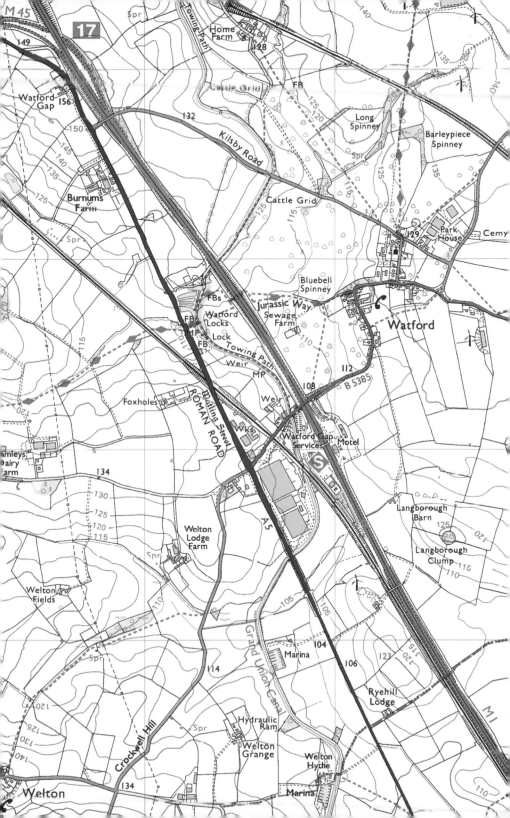

cMap 38 CAVERN CLUB

'Just whatever you do, don't sing.'

We were outside the Cavern Club in Liverpool, the venue which cemented the Beatles' hold over the British music scene in the sixties. There were tourists all around us, and Aunt Bea was clearly afraid I'd startle them into flight. Not that she should have worried. I had absolutely no intention of making an embarrassment of myself.

'The Cavern has moved around a little over the decades, my boy, but it's back more or less where it started – as close as structural safety will allow, anyway. Its creation was inspired by the jazz cellar clubs of Paris, and its founder was Alan Sytner, the son of a prominent local doctor. In 1957, when it started, it was strictly a jazz venue, and on one memorable occasion, John Lennon, who then fronted the Quarrymen, was passed a note mid-set telling him to "cut out the rock 'n roll".

'The Beatles catapulted the club to global fame in the early sixties when the Beatlemania wave hit. For many, they remain the lasting symbol of that decade. There is a simplistic narrative around the post war years in Britain however, and especially the sixties. We think of counterculture, flamboyant clothes, the rise of the much-needed rights movements, alternative thinking, new forms of music, and so on.

'It's all a lot more complicated than that, of course. The Second World War had greatly weakened the remains of the old order, and after a decade or more of austerity, the economy was bouncing back. The children of the post-war baby boom were just coming of age, and they'd had enough of grim depression. New domestic technologies were busy changing daily life, and the middle class was exploding in size. It was a revolution no less profound than any of the squabbles between kings.

'The Beatles crashed into that heady brew, a band of clean-cut local lads in conversation with the music coming out of the African-American community – skiffle, rock 'n roll, rhythm 'n blues... They became the living symbol of this paradigm shift, the inevitable rebalancing of the social order after the grotesque failures of the 1940s. In a sense, it was inevitable that they would split up as the decade ended.

'The Cavern's history hasn't always been easy. It may have been the nest that the decade fledged from, but it was closed down in the early '70s when British Rail forced it out, and again, after it had re-opened, by financial troubles in the '80s. But like Liverpool itself, it's bounced back time and again, and it's been going from strength to strength since the '90s. Make no mistake, my boy. It may not have crenulations or a moat, but The Cavern is a castle, and one as influential as any.

'Now let's find a cup of tea in one of these establishments, and try solving a puzzle or two.'

■ Easy

1. How many ways to cross the river are shown on the map?

2. Where on the map can you find the letters RAN near the letters AIL?

■ Medium

3. What total do you come to if you add up the last digits of each of the B-road numbers printed on the map?

4. The circle that has its centre at the intersection of the arms of the blue cross marking the cathedral and that passes through the location of the U-Boat Story also passes through which common man's name?

■ Tricky

5. Which location sounds like somewhere to go if you felt like a moon walk?

6. With respect to the map, which of the following is the odd one out: 17, 18, 19 or 20?

■ Challenging

7. How many unique examples are there of complete words on the map which are also common verbs in the infinitive form (ie. 'Run', 'Hide', 'Escape', etc.)?

8. Make a note of each of the following six numerical values observed from the map:

   a. The number of places of worship further north on the map than the word 'Vauxhall'.

   b. The lowest number identifying an A-road.

   c. The survey height nearest to the edge of the map.

   d. The number of museums, art galleries and leisure and recreation centres.

   e. The number of times the word Toll appears on the map.

   f. The number of words on the map that are also types of religious building.

   Using each of these six numbers exactly once, performing only the elemental mathematical operations – addition, subtraction, multiplication and division – can you arrive at a total of exactly 800?

River Mersey

Lock

Nelson
Dock

Victoria
Tower

Trafalgar Dock

A5036

A525

Vauxhall

A5054

Sch

Sch

Coll

Schs

Sch

A59

A5038

A5053

Univ

A5046

Pol Sta

A5373

A580

29

Kingsway
(Road Tunnel) Toll

Waterloo
River Entrance

FB

Locks

Princes Dock

B5188

FERRY
SHIP
Douglas

Seacombe Ferry P

Hotels

Lock
6

Royal Liver
Building

Moorfields
Sta

Offices

Univ
Libr

Univ
Hall

A5047

Hotel

Lime St
Station

TH

James St
Station

A525

Twr

A5038

A5339

Central
Sta

Queensway
Mersey Tunnel (Toll)

Pier Head Ferry P

Tunnel

FB

The Fact
Centre

Woodside Ferry P

7

Trans-Pennine Trail

A5040

Sch

Chinese
Arch

Coll

U-boat
Story

FERRIES
SHIP
Belfast
Douglas (Winter)

Albert
Dock

i

ACC

CATHEDRAL

A5038

A5037

A5036

A562

22

MHW

Docks

Office

Mud &
Sand

MHW

Marina

Priory

Toxteth

Map 39 WEMBLEY

'I have always rather taken issue with the characterisation of football as just 22 men chasing a ball around a field. It seems to me that most things can be dismissed in similar ways – ballet is just wiry people jumping, painting is just the daubing of pigment on material and antiques are just old chunks of wood or porcelain. There's a lot of very heavy lifting hiding in that 'just', my boy. Besides, however little interest one may have in watching sport, it's vitally important to the culture at large. Disliking it is perfectly fine. Dismissing it out of hand is, honestly, sheer ignorance.

'George Orwell once referred to serious sport as "war minus the shooting" and it's an insight as profoundly important as anything you'll find in the pages of *1984* or *Animal Farm*. He very much did not approve, but the truth is that all societies need ritualised expressions of rivalry and competition – why else would they all have developed them? Humans have been playing competitive games with various round objects for four thousand years, and the oldest evidence of sporting activity we know of so far goes back to the Lascaux cave paintings fifteen thousand years ago.

'Sporting competition has, we think, always been a way to identify and train the individuals most capable of surviving dangerous physical tasks – warfare, hunting, January sales, and so on – without the risk of causing them harm. It serves many complex roles now in modern society of course, but at this moment I'm particularly interested in one important football match played here in 1966.

'The Second World War had ended just 21 years before, and memories of it were still fiercely strong. The Cold War was rapidly heating up too, and the 1966 FIFA World Cup was a tense affair. Having the very best of England and West Germany squaring up against each other in the final was profoundly symbolic, despite West Germany's status as allies in the new Europe. Add in linesmen from the USSR and a Swiss referee, and you had a very heady continental mix. Then England won in that deeply dramatic fashion, and the match became a mythic touchstone of English sporting pride. That was more than fifty years ago and, so far, it remains the most-watched sporting event in national history. We haven't recaptured that footballing success yet, but we did eventually make it to another major tournament final in 2021.

'Although history would probably be much the same right now if West Germany had won the match, rightly or wrongly that final remains one of the most profoundly important events in the English national psyche. It's not only wars and leaders and that shape nations, my boy. That's something you forget at your peril. You have some questions for us, I trust?'

■ Easy

1. Which full or partial grid row contains the most footbridges?

2. How many times does the word Wembley appear on the map?

■ Medium

3. Which educational establishment is nearest to the edge of the map?

4. Where on the map can you find a Tube station near a route suitable for Ramblers?

■ Tricky

5. How many times does the map show rail bridges crossing above other features?

6. Which location's name contains a word that is one letter change away from being a word that means 'less good'?

■ Challenging

7. Using only capital letters printed in the top row of the map grid, can you find an eight-letter word for a type of alcohol?

8. Can you piece these fragments back together to make four locations shown on the map: ARK, BR, BRI, DGE, EST, FR, GEP, HO, ID, ITE, ON, ONE, OUN, PA, PR, RK, RSE, ST, TC, TRY, WH, YEN?

Map 40 SNOWDON

We were standing by a beautiful lake that nestled between golden-looking hills, with craggy mountains rearing up around us. Behind us, a low, grey, ivy-covered building – the Pen-y-Gwyrd Hotel and mountain rescue post is, I gather, something of a famous landmark with climbers – stood like a sentinel against the landscape, clustered in a shield of trees. It was a truly magical moment.

'You must forgive me some artistic license, my boy. I wanted to finish our trip through time here, in this most beautiful, ancient and unspoilt of landscapes. But I have good reason. Sometimes, the path of history leads people to believe that things were natural or fixed. That events could not have happened another way. What I want to show is that history is made up of an unimaginable number of stories, choices and lives. Time is a tapestry, one that is continually being knitted together, and for all the pomp and bluster of our human society, the truth is that we exist in a sea of chances held together by narratives that we pick out to please ourselves after the fact.

'Out here, surrounded by wild beauty and unforgiving stone, it is easy to see how the chance turning of a rock underfoot can be the difference between seemingly easy success and disastrous failure. We think we've tamed the world, but that's a lie. There is nothing tame about Eryri – Snowdownia, as we English call it. When you look at these peaks, you're looking at the truth of history, mighty and unforgiving. But even that is a lie of sorts, for

these rocks themselves are the victims of chance, thrust high into the air four hundred and fifty million years ago, and have steadily eroded ever since.

'Not that we're powerless, you understand. In 1967, Esmé Kirby founded *Cymdeithas Eryri* (the Snowdonia Society), with her husband Peter, for the express purpose of protecting these amazing peaks from human despoilment and development. Esmé had been carefully farming sheep in this valley, Dyffryn Mymbyr, for thirty years, and even left the 2,500 acre estate to the National Trust in her will. The Society has gone from strength to strength, watch-dogging both businesses and conservation efforts in their care of the mountains as well as removing litter, keeping footpaths navigable and safeguarding wildlife.

'Take any point in the past and it is like any other moment in time – complex, confusing, ruled by random happenstance as much as the morass of competing intents, with all manner of unanticipated consequence. History, however, is a story, a narrative pulled together to tell a tale. We think it means that the present is somehow solid or inevitable, but that's just not true. A story, remember? Many challenges lie ahead of us, and if we're going to weather them, we need to pull our socks up.

'But enough of that. How about some puzzles in the Hotel's bar to finish off with? I hear their quiche is quite good.'

Easy

1. How many waterfalls and named lakes are shown on the map?

2. What is the lowest height printed on the map?

Medium

3. What is the elevation of the contour line that passes between the 'e' and 'n' of the Hotel's name?

4. Which location sounds like part of a goat?

Tricky

5. Which full or partial square of the map grid contains numbers that add up to a total of 4,830, starting with 1A at the top left, numbers increasing downwards and letters increasing to the right?

6. Ignoring punctuation, how many locations on the map contain the letters G, W and Y adjacent but in any order?

Challenging

7. The circle that has its centre at the crossroads on The Miner's Track and passes through the peak of Glyder Fawr also passes through the entire length of which word?

8. Which two place names can be combined to form the anagram FAREWELL, PART ANGLICAN?

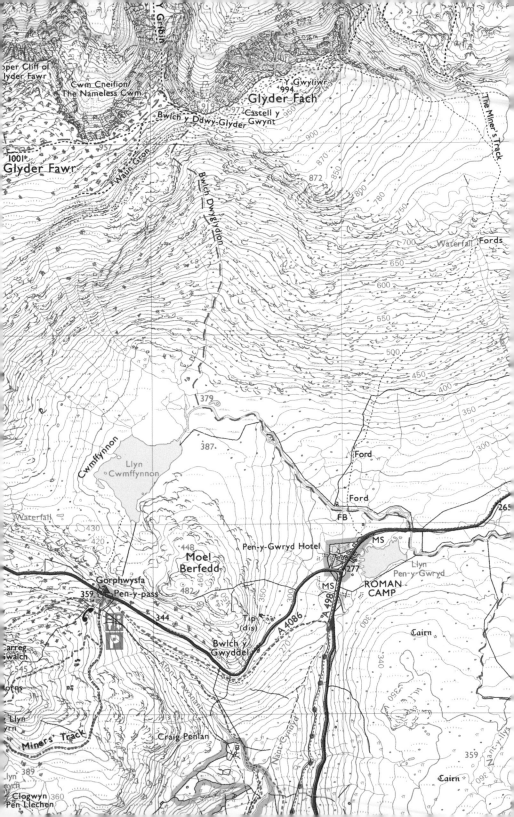

Solutions

MAP

I

1. Caravan/camping (west of Happisburgh).

2. Three (White's Farm, Gold's Farm, Green Farm).

3. Short Lane ('Snort').

4. Twenty-four (Church Farm, White's Farm, Gold's Farm, Lighthouse Farm, Thompson's Farm, Littlewood Farm, Seacroft Farm, Manor Farm, Hall Farm, Holly Farm, Green Farm, Lower Farm, Mill Farm, College Farm, Moat Farm, Barneys Farm, Whittleton's Farm, Thirsts Farm, Willow Farm, Church Farm Road, Moat Farm, Church Farm, Manor Farm, Grange Farm).

5. Manor, because it also appears in the name of a location that is not identified as a farm (The Manor).

6. England (England Coast Path).

7. a. Fern House, b. Seacroft Farm, c. Cart Gap Road, d. Grub Street.

8. The Manor at Lessingham. (Lighthouse at Lighthouse Farm east to the coast by England Coast Path, follow south to telephone at Inflatable Rescue Boat Station, head west to crossroads near Lower Farm, south to telephone near Church Farm, follow road west to Oak north of Manor Farm, and head north past 'Coronation' to 'Manor'. The most easterly incidence of 'Manor' on the map is The Manor.)

MAP
2

1. Middle Down Drove.

2. Swallow Hole.

3. Six (Mascall's Wood, Bubwith Acres Nature Reserve, Middledown Nature Reserve, and unnamed reserves near Rhino Rift, Black Rock and Batcombe Hollow).

4. A valley.

5. Jacob's Ladder.

6. Greater (70 degrees).

7. Black Rock and Wind Rock.

8. 252 (Middle Down Drove) + 138 (near Sow's Hole) + 188 (north of Carscliff Farm) = 578.

MAP
3

1. Four (West of Gernos-fach, south of Garfeth, south-west of Mynydd-du Commin, east of the Tumulus).

2. 5D (536m at the triangulation pillar on Foel Cwmcerwyn).

3. Sheepfolds (disused), with seventeen letters.

4. Banc Du ('Bank, do').

5. Foel Cwmcerwyn is further.

6. Four (195m on contour line south of Penanty-isaf to the southern spring just off the B4329 at Rhyd-y-groes).

7. Carn Fach and Pen Cisty.

8. Castell-y-cynhen, Bwlch Pennant, Mynydd-du Commin, Standing Stones. (Each line is one location. All punctuation is removed, and then every letter is replaced with the one immediately following it in the alphabet, so A becomes B, etc.)

MAP
4

1. Two (Ebbsfleet Lane and Cottington Road).

2. Cliffsend Point.

3. Two (A256 and A299 twice).

4. Energy Park.

5. 3 (South of Shell Ness), 9 (Patch of woodland southwest of Ebbsfleet).

6. Five (St Augustine's Well, Pegwell Bay, Sandwich & Pegwell Bay National Nature Reserve, Pegwell Bay Country Park and Shell Ness).

7. Point. It is the only one not appearing in association with St. Augustine.

8. Traditional, Sevenscore, Canterbury, Richborough.

MAP
5

1. North of Wensum Park.

2. The Cow Tower.

3. The castle.

4. Right (two: one south-west of Gas Hill, one east of Trowse Millgate).

5. Boudicca Way.

6. A1242. It is the only one that does not pass close by to a school.

7. Mousehold Heath ('Household').

8. 270. $(1402+2)/4-(39+42) = 270$; the A1402 south of Philadelphia, two blue numbers along the top edge, four museums, 39m road height SE of Gas Hill, and 42m height at Mousehold Heath.

MAP
6

1. A picnic spot and a walk/trail (Donview).

2. 529m (aerial survey point at Oxen Craig).

3. Overton (the Overton window, also known as the window of discourse, which says that there is a fixed size to the spread of political viewpoints the public will tolerate).

4. B5, with eleven words.

5. 161m aerial survey height at Overton Wood.

6. Tap. It is the only one appearing on the map in black.

7. Millstone Hill.

8. 110m (second 5m contour line up from the 104m ground survey point at Upper Woodend).

MAP
7

1. 112 (10 + 20 + 25 + 29 + 28 = 112).

2. Longburgh (Cattle grid, Longburgh Farm).

3. West End.

4. Eighteen.

5. Watch Hill ('Witch').

6. Sands does not appear in the same word as 'burgh'.

7. a. Milecastle, b. Ridding Sough, c. Amberfield, d. Mean High Water.

8. Holy Well Wood (From West End school, north to the 20m contour near the triangulation pillar, west to the footpath north of the disused butts, then south to the end near the sewage works, and south-east to the end of the woodland southeast of Shield Farm, then south to Holy Well Wood.)

MAP
8

1. Six (north-east of Bwlch, south of Beggar's Bush, west and south-west of Court Farm, south-west of Burfa Bog Nature Reserve, and at the south-west corner of the map).

2. Just north of Beggar's Bush Farm (between 265m and 270m).

3. Lower House (closer than Yew Tree Farm or Mound).

4. The bottom left complete square, around Knobley.

5. Seven: plantation (e.g. Lower Chandlers Plantation), wood (e.g. Benbow Wood), copse (Granner Copse), thorn (Thorn), bush (Beggar's Bush), and tree and yew (Yew Tree Farm).

6. Discoed.

7. Court Farm. (From Castlering Wood head north to the road, then north again to the well at Middle House. Follow the footpath to the church at Discoed and then north to the road and follow west to the crossroads with the B4357. Jump from the 194m survey to the 198m survey at Evenjobb. Court Farm is directly south-west.)

8. Subtract the number of wells (f, 7) from the second-highest survey point (a, 337m at Granner Wood) to get 330. Divide this by the number of farms (d, 5) to get 66. Add the number of letters in the longest location name (b, 24, tied between Upper and Lower Chandlers Plantation) to get 90. Subtract that 90 from the lowest height on the map (e, 165m printed on a contour line near the top right) to get 75. Finally, multiply that by the number of times 'Burfa' appears (c, 4) to hit 300.

MAP
9

1. The area of Layerthorpe known as Foss Islands (just west of the word 'York').

2. 18m (west of the bicycle hire facility and south-west of the National Railway Museum).

3. Germany (Germany Beck).

4. Millennium Bridge.

5. Eight (east of Micklegate Stray, north of Nunthorpe, south of the Castle, west of Foss Islands, south and north-east of Layerthorpe, and two south of Heworth).

6. A short way east of the B1227, north of the Castle.

7. Five (Racecourse, Barracks, Ebvracvm, Scarcroft, AR Centre).

8. Hospitium, Scarcroft, Clementhorpe, Nature.

MAP
10

1. 44m (in Great Wood).

2. Four (south of Battle Abbey Farm, north of Peppering Eye Farm, east of Stumblet's Wood and south of the pump house).

3. 4,466 (A271+B2095+A2100).

4. They all appear within the names of farms (Moorbank Farm, Coarsebarn Farm, Little Park Farm and Brakes Coppice Farm).

5. Crowhurst.

6. Camel (C from Coarsebarn Farm or Coppice Farm; A from Battle Abbey Farm; M from Moorbank Farm or Millers Farm; E from Peppering Eye Farm; L from Loose Farm or Little Park Farm).

7. Fore Wood Nature Reserve. (Head north from the museum in Battle to the windmill and adjacent 107m pillar north-west of Caldbec Hill. Jump to the 117m aerial survey height on the road north of Telham Place and follow the road west to the 98m road survey height east of Telham Hill then straight west to the spring south of Lower Telham and south to the destination.)

8. a. Powder Mills Hotel, b. Stonequarry Wood, c. Telham Lane, d. Horselodge Plantation.

MAP
11

1. Four (south of Oxford Canal Walk, two north of Osney Bridge, and west of Thames Path).

2. Five (Marston Brook, Oxford Canal, Peasmoor Brook, Bulstake Stream and Hinksey Stream).

3. (A)420 + (B)480 + (B)4495 = 5,395.

4. The 63m survey point.

5. Brook ('Crook').

6. St Catherine (St Catherine's College).

7. Osney and Jericho.

8. Hogacre Ditch, River Cherwell, Lady Margaret Hall, Cold Harbour. (The location names are run together with spaces removed, then the text is reversed and broken into groups of six letters. The last two letters of the last block are dummy text to fill out a whole group.)

MAP
12

1. Eight (B3021, A328, B376, A308, A30, B3407, B388, M25).

2. John F Kennedy Memorial.

3. Runnymede House.

4. The third row down, with five ground survey heights (73m, 83m, 68m, 18m and 16m).

5. Parking (three locations).

6. The University east of Englefield Green, in the shape of an eight.

7. Fosters. It is the only one that only appears once on the map.

8. Nine. (Beaumont FARM, Sailing CLUB, Hythe END, Runnymede HOUSE, LOCK, Runnymede PARK, PRUNE Hill, South LODGE Farm, RESEARCH Laboratories. Uncommon/obscure verbs on the map include 'path', 'island', 'hill', 'coll', 'lane', 'weir', 'river', etc., and there are several verbs that are not in the infinitive, such as 'sailing' and 'springs'.)

MAP
13

1. One (Leitchland Farm).

2. Barskiven Hill, on the east edge.

3. Eleven (four around Linwood, five to the north of Quarrelton, one south of Quarrelton, and one to the north-west of Elderslie).

4. Highcraig Wood, at 130m.

5. Newton Wood (Sir Isaac Newton).

6. Cemy, north of Elderslie.

7. Low Bardrain. (From the mast north-west of Phoenix Business Park, head west to the roundabout south of Linwood then south to the residential area between the two minor roads south-east of the train station. Head east to the school east of Elderslie, then north to the B-road and follow the B789 to the T-junction north-east of Elderslie. Head south on the yellow road and stay on the road past the left-hand turn after Glenpatrick. Second right then takes you to Low Bardrain.)

8. 65. There are 9 schools (3 west of Linwood, 2 near Linwood, 1 east of Linwood, 1 north-east of Quarrelton, 1 by Elderslie and 1 by Johnstone); 4 instances of 'weir' or 'weirs' (west of the sewage works, north of the river near the western edge of the map, north of Leitchland Farm and south of Leitchland Farm); 24 letters in the longest place name [High Craig Quarry (Whinstone), noting that the brackets are not counted as letters]; 125 is the highest printed contour line elevation (south of Old Patrick Water); 75 printed in red (south-east of Linwood); 1 Park and Ride (north-east of Quarrelton); and 6 is the lowest aerial survey location, north of the sewage works). Then $9 + 4 - 1 = 12$; $24 \div 12 = 2$; $2 \times 125 = 250$; $250 + 75 = 325$; $6 - 1 = 5$, and $325 \div 5 = 65$.

MAP
14

1. Bincleaves Groyne ('Bin cleave groin').

2. South-east of The Ridgeway Centre.

3. Two (The Oceanarium and the fishing facilities at the south end of Radipole Lake).

4. There are five sites labelled 'hide' (three at Radipole Lake Nature Reserve and two at Lodmoor Country Park).

5. Hardy Way (Thomas Hardy).

6. The Landing Stage.

7. Nine (Lodmoor Country Park, Southill, South West Coast Path, Weymouth Bay, Weymouth, South Pier, Harbour, Southlands, Portland Harbour).

8. a. Melcombe Regis, b. Sandsfoot Castle, c. South West Coast Path, d. Commercial Pier.

MAP
15

1. Two (north of St. James's and south-east of Belgravia).

2. The (Kia) Oval.

3. A literal 'May fair', a rural fair held in May which was what the area was famed for until the mid eighteenth century.

4. Sixteen (seven bridges – Waterloo, Hungerford, Westminster, Lambeth, Vauxhall, Grosvenor and Chelsea; plus nine museums – south-east of Bond Street, north-west of the Strand, west of the Royal Academy, south of Trafalgar Square, west of Green Park, south of the Government Offices, south of St. James's Park, east of Westminster Bridge and north-east of Lambeth Bridge).

5. There is no Leicester House shown on the map.

6. South of the Millennium Arena.

7. Battersea Power Station, Houses of Parliament, Hungerford Bridge and Royal Festival Hall.

8. Spotless (SP from St James's Park, O from Oval, T from Temple, E from Embankment, LS from Leicester Square, and S from Bond Street).

MAP
16

1. Hope Monument on Airngath Hill, top right corner.

2. Williamcraigs Farm at seventeen letters.

3. The bottom partial row with five (134m north of Williamcraigs, 113m north-east of Williamcraigs Farm, 115m east of Preston Dam, 141m east of Upper Glen, 124m north of Hiltly).

4. The centre of the cemetery.

5. 74 is the only one that does not appear on the map.

6. We selected 803 from the A803, 706 from the A706, 171 from the aerial survey point on Airngath Hill, and 120 from any one of half a dozen contour line heights. 803+754+171+72=1800.

7. Waterfall. (From Mine (dis) in the top left corner, head east to Mile End and turn south to Gardners Hall. From there, head to the A706 and the 77m aerial survey height, then the train station and nearby minor road T-junction near the museum and boat hire, and proceed south-west to Subway, north of Preston Glen. Waterfall is the first word printed to the south of Subway.)

8. Mount Michael and Grange.

MAP
17

1. Stratford-upon-Avon Racecourse, at twenty-seven letters.

2. No public house is shown on the map.

3. The Obelisk in Welcombe Hills Country Park.

4. Bluecap Covert.

5. Four (A439, a narrow stretch of road south of Lodge, B4086 and a minor road north of Playing Fields).

6. Greater (a little over 35 degrees).

7. Four – Cross (O' the Hill Farm), Church (Farm), Temple (Hill), Bishop(ton).

8. Hopscotch (HO from Orchard Hill Cottages, P from Welcombe Hills Country Park, SC from Stony Hill Covert, and OTCH from Cross O' The Hill Farm).

MAP
18

1. The ferry path south of The Sound.

2. The column to the right of centre, with eight (two east of Ford, one north of Milehouse, one west of Stoke, one west and two south of Victoria Park, and one east of the Marina).

3. Three (Dockyard Station and Devonport Station on the train line, and the Lifeboat and Inshore Rescue Boat Station at West Hoe).

4. The raven (The Raven's Cliffs / Ravenness Point)

5. A burial mound or tumulus.

6. Mutton Cove ('Button').

7. Devonport Station. (Head south on orange road near top left, east on yellow road, south-east at crossroads, to junction south-west of cathedral and turn west, keep west on to A374, then turn east onto yellow road south-west of Devonport Park, turn north-east north of The Brickfields, west at the church, and south over the train line to Devonport Station.)

8. Empacombe and Central Park.

MAP
19

1. Five.

2. 50m (contour line in a patch of woodland south-east of Rainbow Hill).

3. 4, appearing 31 times. (Counting full and partial grid squares from top left, numbering rows and lettering columns: 1A: 0, 1B: 1, 1C: 0, 1D: 2, 2A: 0, 2B: 3, 2C: 3, 2D: 1, 3A: 1, 3B: 15, 3C: 2, 3D: 0, 4A: 1, 4B: 1, 4C: 1, 3D: 0, 5A: 0, 5B: 0, 5C: 0, 5D: 0.)

4. Rainbow Hill.

5. The college building east of St John's (an 'E').

6. Cricket Ground and Duck Brook. (There's also 'fish' partially printed south-west of Manor Farm, and although types of butterfly are very specific, you may also count Monarch's Way.)

7. University, Barbourne, Racecourse, Manor Farm. (Each line is one location. Any spaces are removed and then the vowels, including Y, are replaced with the letter immediately before them in the alphabet, wrapping to replace A with Z. Consonants are left unchanged.)

8. Bromwich Parade Path, Pitchcroft Recn Gd, Three Choirs Way, Worcester Bridge.

MAP
20

1. Three (St Luke, St Paul, St Katharine).

2. 16m (ground survey point south-west of Farringdon Station).

3. Two (one north of Aldgate East, one west of the Globe Theatre).

4. Spitalfields Market.

5. Monument.

6. London Bridge is the only one of these stations which has the word 'Station' spelled out in full rather than abbreviated.

7. (A)501+(A)201+(A)201 = 903. (There are three instances of A201 printed on the map; any two are acceptable.)

8. a. Blackfriars Pier, b. Aldgate East, c. Elephant and Castle, d. Shoreditch.

MAP
21

1. The B4066 at Berkeley.

2. Five (at Hook Street, Hamfield Lane, at Brownsmill Farm, by the telephone at Ham, and at Pedington Farm).

3. 19m aerial survey height east of Berkeley Station.

4. One (Westfield Brake).

5. Oakhunger.

6. 21 is the only one that appears in black.

7. The moat east of Doverte Brook.

8. Floodgates Farm, Matford Bridge, Whitcliff Park and Berkeley Station.

MAP
22

1. Diana Princess of Wales Memorial Walk, at thirty-two letters.

2. Three (B507, B319 and B310).

3. They all appear on the map as part of the name of a district of London (St John's Wood, Marylebone and Mayfair).

4. 3B, the square containing Lisson Grove, with nine places of worship.

5. 38 only appears on the map once (as part of the A4380), whilst the others all appear multiply.

6. Mornington Crescent.

7. Lord's. (From the Science Museum in Knightsbridge go to the Royal Albert Hall, then east along the A315 and A4 to Green Park. Turn into Mayfair on the light orange road, then head north-east at the square in Mayfair (Berkeley Square) to the pink road (Regent Street), and then north-north-east to the Tube station (Regent St. Tube). Proceed straight west to the Tube station symbol at Paddington, and from there to the recreation centre east of Paddington. Then move north to the mosque in Regent's Park, and west to Lord's Cricket Ground.)

8. Great Portland Street, The Serpentine, Rotten Row and Madame Tussauds.

MAP

23

1. Nine (Hyde Hill Plantation, Kimber's Copse, Ashe Park Copse, Round Wood, Berrydown Copse, Quintan's Plantation, Stubb's Copse, West Wood, Crawley Copse).

2. Pit (dis) and Pits (dis) in eleven locations.

3. Oak (i.e. Oakley Hall) and Ash (i.e. Ashe Park).

4. Six. (The contour you cross at the railway line doubles back and you then cross it again.)

5. The 99m point on the B3400 at Manor Farm.

6. Rage does not appear with a location name on the map (Nurshanger Farm, Folly Farm, Itchen Row and Steventon).

7. Steventon Arch, thirteen letters.

8. Ash Park and Berrydown Copse or Ash Park Copse and Berrydown.

MAP

24

1. Two (south of Sinclairtown, south of Port Brae).

2. Mitchelston Industrial Estate, at twenty-seven letters.

3. 981 − 78 = 903 (B981 at West Gallatown, 78m ground survey height south of West Gallatown).

4. Pathhead is the only name that is not close to a school.

5. Five (golf course north of Garden Wood, walk or trail east of Garden Wood, ice rink at West Gallatown, walk or trail west of Ravenscraig Park, recreation / leisure / sports centre west of Fife Coastal Path). Note: you may also count the go-karting east of Mitchelston Industrial Estate as a sixth location if you like.

6. Twelve (school south of Playing Field, school south-east of Hayfield, school north of cemetery, college and university south-west of Port Brae, school west of Linktown, schools (count as two) east of Smeaton, school south-west of Sinclairtown, school north of Port Brae, school east of West Gallatown, school south-west of Windmill.)

7. a: Kirkcaldy Sands, b: Sinclairtown, c: Randolph Road, d: Craig-endle.

8. The windmill. (From Dovecot, west to the place of worship south of Hayfield, then minor roads south then west to yellow road and follow that south to the junction south-east of the cemetery. The museum symbol is pointing to the library. Go from there to the train track. Keep north on the train tracks to the crossing with B928. The windmill is to the north-west.)

MAP
25

1. Six (Gravelhill, Round Hill, Gravel Hill Farm, Gravel Hill Lane, Coton Hill and Porthill).

2. The place of worship north of the garden centre.

3. B4386 (south-west of Frankwell).

4. Two (Kingsland Bridge, Kingsland).

5. 72 does not appear as part of a road number.

6. The paths of the cemetery north-east of Meole Brace.

7. Seven. (From hospital, head north-east to A-road south-west of abbey and turn left (1). At the T-junction south of school, turn left again (2). Follow that road to the T-junction at the market (3) and either turn right, then quickly left and right north-west of the castle (6) or turn left, then right at Shire Hall, and right again before the river (6). Follow that road to the 58m aerial survey height and turn right to the school (7).)

8. Mountfields and Kingsland.

MAP
26

1. One (west of Stanford on Soar).

2. None.

3. The leftmost, with three.

4. South of Loughborough.

5. Lock (to Dock).

6. Three (Mead – Bishop's Meadow Nature Reserve and Loughborough Meadows, Ale – Industrial Estate).

7. Cubic. (CU: Grand Union Canal; B: Summerpool Brook or Hermitage Brook; IC: Indoor Climbing Centre.)

8. Stanford on Soar, Belton Park, Shelthorpe and AR Centre. (Starting at the bottom left of the block, the location names are written upwards.)

MAP
27

1. East of Close House.

2. Eleven (from west to east, 160, 125, 140, 130, 125, 120, 120, 115, 120, 110, 115).

3. Telephones – four (at Eldon, Eldon Lane, the eastern industrial estate and near the football grounds).

4. 97m (south of South Church).

5. Middridge Grange Mill.

6. 163 + 168 + 162 = 493. (All three are ground survey heights, near Eldon Blue House, west of Old Eldon and west of New House.)

7. The words viCARage (The Old Vicarage) and CARaVAN (Caravan Site).

8. Nine (CLOSE House, Eldon BLUE House, SOUTH Church, The OLD Vicarage, GREEN Lane, INDUSTRIAL Estate, NEW Shildon, EAST Thickley, RED House Beck.)

MAP
28

1. Eight (Seal Gut, Craford's Gut, Middin Gut, Piper Gut, St Cuthbert's Gut, Churn Gut, Wideopen Gut and Scarcar Gut).

2. The 17m aerial survey height at the lighthouse on Inner Farne.

3. Callers.

4. Wamses (Ramses).

5. Sunderland Hole.

6. Twenty-eight (four near Knivestone, eleven in the large group, two at Gun Rock, six near Callers and five in the duplicated excerpt). Note that Little Scarcar, Big Scarcar and The Bush should not be counted twice.

7. The six numbers are 4, 4, 11, 11, 13, 17. We did it this way: $11 \times 17 = 187$, and $4 \times 4 \times 11 = 176$. $176 + 187 = 363$. $363 - 13 = 350$.

8. Wideopen Gut and Northern Hares.

MAP
29

1. Three (Town Moor, Hunter's Moor and [Nu]ns Moor Park).

2. Tidal Basin south of Dunston Coal Staiths.

3. 77m, at the ground survey points on the A189 near Leazes Park and west of the Civic Centre on the B601.

4. Four (Hunter's Moor, Arthur's Hill, St James' Park and Hadrian's Wall Path).

5. Five (playing field north of Arthur's Hill, St. James' Park stadium, the recreation centre west of Newcastle Central Station, Hadrian's Wall Path trail and the recreation centre east of Bensham).

6. 601 + 193 + 186 = 980 (601 for the B601 north of the Civic Centre, 193 for the A193 south of Shieldfield, 186 for A186 southwest of Battle Field.)

7. Leazes Park. (Start at the museum west of Newcastle Central Station and go north to the A186. Jump to the A186 south of Battle Field. Turn north and continue to the inverted Y-junction at Shieldfield. Move straight north to the cemetery at Jesmond, then take the minor road west to the B1307, and across to Exhibition Park. South-west of that is the lake in Leazes Park.)

8. IMBIBES. (There are multiple sources for several letters, but we used: I from King Edward VII Bridge, MB from Millennium Bridge, IBE from Queen Elizabeth II Bridge, and S from Swing Bridge.)

MAP
30

1. Waterloo Station.

2. The Oval is further.

3. The third row down, with fourteen educational establishments, one more than the row below it.

4. The tube station symbol west of the cathedral at Westminster (This symbol shows the location of Victoria Station tube station which is unnamed on the map).

5. Vauxhall Bridge.

6. They all appear in location names near the river (Charing Cross Station, Royal Festival Hall, Somerset House and The Jewel Tower).

7. Five. (Heading east on the A-road below Buckingham Palace [the A3214 for reference], take the first right and then the first to head east through Westminster, then turn left north of the Abbey [Parliament Square] then immediately right onto the A302, then the second left onto the Embankment to Somerset House.)

8. a: Lambeth Palace, b: Leicester Square, c: River Thames, d: Lancaster House.

MAP
31

1. Three (Whitworth Park, Alexandra Park and Platt Fields Park).

2. The place of worship with a tower north of Ancoats, on the 50m height contour.

3. Whitworth Park.

4. They all appear within location names close to a recreational route.

5. 6469 + 6181 + 5117 = 17,767 (B6469 west of Oxford Road Station, B6181 south-west of Ancoats, B5117 north of Whitworth Park).

6. Platt Fields Park (Plate).

7. We did it this way: 49 x 41 = 2,009; 29 x 33 = 957; 2,009 + 957 = 2,966; 2,966 + 33 = 2,999. (49m north-west of Ancoats, 41m south of Piccadilly Station, 29m west of Whalley Range, 33m south of Deansgate Station and 33m east of Deansgate Station.)

8. Aquatics Centre, Deansgate Station, Cheshire Ring and Rochdale Canal. (Each location is broken up into syllables, and then the letters of each syllable are arranged into alphabetical order. Nothing else is changed. Finally, the spaces are removed, and then the resulting text is broken into blocks of five letters.)

MAP
32

1. Three (Nant-y-croft, Blaen-y-cwm and Nant-y-Bwch).

2. South of Cefn Golau.

3. Two (one at Nant-y-croft and one northwest of Duke's Meadow.)

4. Near the pub in the top right corner of the map, in Nant-y-croft and Subway.

5. The bus station is further.

6. 356 does not appear as a ground survey height.

7. Afon Sirhywi, Sion Sieffre, Scwrfa and Hirgan-fach.

8. Sheepfold and Sirhowy River.

MAP
33

1. A64 south-east of Edgehill.

2. 150m.

3. Four (CLARENCE GarDENs, St NICHOLAS Cliff, ROMAN Signal Station, and OLIVER's Mount.)

4. There are four of each – for sports, the cricket ground, water board activities off South Sands, the recreation and sports centre east of Oliver's Mount, and the Scarborough South Cliff Golf Club; for tourist features, the site at Peasholm Park, The Spa Complex, the Star Disk and The Mere.

5. Betty Muffet Rocks.

6. Superstore (south-east of Woodlands).

7. 27m ground survey north of Northstead, 69m aerial survey south-east of Wheatcroft, and 4m ground survey east of Old Harbour (27 + 69 + 4 = 100).

8. They all appear in locations that have the word Cliff in their name (Scarborough South Cliff Golf Club, South Cliff Gardens and Wheatcroft Cliff).

MAP
34

1. 5m south-west of Jarrow.

2. The Oil Depot north of Jarrow.

3. King George's Field, at sixteen letters.

4. Three (place of worship east of Primrose to Leisure Pool north of Royal Quays, passing through A194, A185 [number partially shown] and the orange dual carriageway).

5. Eight (A193, A187, A19, B1297, A185 [number partially shown], B1516, A194 and A1300).

6. Jarrow Slake (Shake).

7. 76 (2 recreation centres, at top left of page and west of Jarrow; 2 oil/gas facilities, north of Willington Quay and north of Jarrow; lowest A-road number is 19. 2 + 2 = 4; 4 x 19 = 76).

8. a: Tyne Car Terminal, b: River Tyne Trail, c: Playing Field, d: Monastery (rems of).

MAP
35

1. Five (south of Waterfoot Road, south-east and south of Burnhouse, south of Stoneside and north of Kirktonmoor Road).

2. There are four Borlands to three places of worship (Low Borland, Mid Borland, High Borland and Borland Burn; two places of worship in Eaglesham and one north-west of the School at Burnhouse).

3. White Cart Water.

4. They all appear more than once on the map.

5. Five – House, Tower, Farm, Castle and Hotel (i.e. Housecraigs, Tower north of Burnhouse, Windhill Farm west of Waterfoot, Castlehill and Hotel at Eaglesham).

6. Four. (From Bonnyton lane/drive, turn left on Bonnyton Moor Road, right at the roundabout north-east of Castlehill House, left on to the B767 at Eaglesham, and left on to Waterfoot Road at Waterfoot Bridge.)

7. Brackenrig Burn. (From Mearns Castle Golf Academy, south to Waterfoot Road, then from the W follow the 125m contour to the W of Windhill Farm. 145m height is southwest. Jumpt to 145m survey height south of Low Borland. Head approximately north, then west on the A726. Turn north at the mound to the Burn.)

8. Bogside and Townhead of Dripps.

MAP
36

1. 187m ground survey height south of West Creech Hill and 32m air survey height north of Clay Pit.

2. Three (Black Barrow, Whiteway/Whiteway Hill and Gold Down).

3. Barrow, appearing eight times (Black Barrow, Povington Barrow, Thorn Barrow, Water Barrows, Ferny Barrows, Worbarrow, Worbarrow Bay and Worbarrow Tout).

4. Gold Down.

5. North Egliston and Chapel Close, north of Tyneham Great Wood.

6. Five (East Holme Range, West Creech, West Creech Hill, North Egliston and South West Coast Path).

7. DOORMAN (DO and M: MOD, O: Observe, R: Ranges, A: Area, N: Notices).

8. Povington Hill, Black Barrow, Tyneham House and Worbarrow Tout. (Spaces are removed and each letter is replaced with the two-digit number showing that letter's position in the alphabet, so A is 01, B is 02, and on to Z as 26.)

MAP
37

1. The M1.

2. Langborough Clump.

3. Barleypiece Spinney and Watford Gap Services tie for the longest name at eighteen letters.

4. The 156m ground survey height at Watford Gap.

5. Bramleys Dairy Farm.

6. They all appear in location names with at least one word that can be found elsewhere on the map. (Long Spinney > Bluebell Spinney; Welton Lodge Farm > Welton Fields; Roman Road > Kilsby Road).

7. 156m ground survey at Watford Gap, 104m and 106m ground surveys east of Marina, and 134m ground survey either south of Crockwell Hill or east of Bramleys Dairy Farm. 156+104+106+134=500.

8. Ryehill Lodge and Towing Path.

MAP
38

1. Six (two tunnels at the Kingsway Tunnel, Seacombe Ferry, Queensway Tunnel, Pier Head Ferry, unnamed Tunnel [Merseyrail].)

2. Trans Pennine Trail.

3. 3 + 7 + 9 = 19 (B5173 east of the police station, B5187 north-west of Moorfields Station and B5339 north-west of Central Station).

4. Douglas.

5. Spaceport

6. 20 does not appear on the map, either on its own or as part of a larger number (B5173, B5187 and 19m ground survey height north-west of Moorfields Station).

7. 11: Lock, Dock, Toll, Tower, Stage, Station, Trail, Arch, Tunnel, Ferry and Ship.

8. The numbers are:

a: 4 (east of Vauxhall near map edge, northeast of Vauxhall and north of the school, east of the A59, and east of Nelson Dock),

b: 41 from the A41 near the bottom left,

c: 7 from 7m ground survey point east of the most northerly Lock,

d: 8 (one leisure centre in the north-east of the map, one university and one art gallery at the University, one museum at the town ball, and three museums and an art gallery near Albert Dock, for a total of 8),

e: 3, twice on tunnels across the river and once to the west of the Priory,

f: 2, Cathedral and Priory.

We reached 800 this way: 7*8=56. 56+41=97. 97+3=100. 100*2=200. 200*4=800.

MAP
39

1. The fourth row down, with seven (counting the FBs north of the Power Station as two bridges).

2. Four (Wembley Park, Wembley Stadium, Wembley Arena, Wembley Central Tube station).

3. School east of Fryent Country Park.

4. South of Preston, where the recreational route passes by Preston Road.

5. Twelve (one south and one west of Alperton, four at Brent Junction and Stonebridge Park, two north-west of Wembley Central, one south of B4557, one west of Academy, one east of Preston Road and one south-east of Preston).

6. White Horse Bridge ('Worse').

7. SCHNAPPS. (S: Sch, C: Fryent Country Park, H: Barn Hill, N: Nursery, A: A4140, P: Preston, P: Preston Road, S: Barn Hill Open Space.)

8. White Horse Bridge, Stonebridge Park, Fryent Country Park and Preston.

MAP
40

1. Five (waterfall west of Fords, Llyn Cwmffynnon, waterfall north-west of Gorphwysfa, Llyn Pen-y-Gwryd and Llyn Teyrn).

2. 265m at the ground survey point near the east edge of the map.

3. 380m (it passes between 379m and 387m survey heights north-east of Llyn Cwmffynnon and is two lines below a 400m contour indicator west of Nant Ddu).

4. The Horns.

5. 2C, starting with 1A at the top left, and with numbers increasing downwards and letters increasing to the right (800 + 780 + 750 + 700 + 650 + 600 + 550 = 4,830, all numbers on contour lines).

6. Eight (Y Gwyliwr, Bwlch y Ddwy-Glyder, Castell y Gwynt, Bwlch Dwyglydion, Pen-y-Gwyrd Hotel, Llyn Pen-y-Gwyrd, Bwlch y Gwyddel and Clogwyn Pen Llechen).

7. Llyn (of Llyn Pen-y-Gwyrd).

8. Waterfall and Craig Penlan.

NOTES

NOTES

ORDNANCE SURVEY MAP INFORMATION

The Ordnance Survey Great British Treasure Hunt features our celebrated OS Explorer mapping, enlarged slightly from the familiar scale of 1:25 000 to 1:20 000 to improve the puzzle experience. The iconic OS Explorer Map is used daily by thousands of people, from ramblers to rock climbers. The first time maps were produced at the 1:25 000 scale (2½ inches on the map being equivalent to 1 mile on the ground, or 4cm to 1km) was in the early twentieth century, but back then only the military had access to this level of detail on a paper map; the first military map from Ordnance Survey covered East Anglia.

Mapping was extremely important during the two world wars, but it wasn't until 1938 that it was suggested that a series of maps be produced for the general public. The thinking was that if this idea took off in schools, then the mapping might eventually cover the whole of Great Britain to give outdoors enthusiasts unrivalled access to the countryside. The first experimental (or Provisional) maps at this scale appeared after the Second World War ended in 1945.

Interest in leisure time spent in the countryside began to grow, and more consideration was given to 1:25 000 mapping. In 1972 the first Outdoor Leisure (OL) map was published, of the Dark Peak area of the Peak District, and subsequently other OL maps were published, concentrating on the national parks and areas of outstanding natural beauty. As a result of the success of the Outdoor Leisure maps, many other maps were redesigned. These were called Pathfinders, and they covered England and Wales, showing all public rights of way and making it easier to plan walking routes.

The first OS Explorer maps were published in 1994, replacing the popular Pathfinder series and making our maps even more user-friendly. On average the OS Explorer maps covered three times the area of the Pathfinders and were six times bigger than the original Outdoor Leisure maps at this scale. The additional tourist and leisure information – including viewpoints, pubs, picnic sites – resulted in an amazing level of detail.

By 2003, every Pathfinder and Outdoor Leisure map had been converted to the OS Explorer series and in 2004, following the Countryside and Rights of Way Act 2000, areas of open access were depicted. These days, if you buy an OS Explorer map you also get a free mobile download to use in our award-winning OS Maps app.

Not sure which leisure map you need for your next adventure? Here's a handy comparison:

OS Explorer 1:25 000 (4cm to 1km or 2½ inches to the mile)

OS Explorer is the nation's most popular leisure map. It features footpaths, rights of way and open-access land, and is recommended for walking, running and horse riding. The OS Explorer map covers a smaller area than the OS Landranger map, but presents the landscape in more detail, aiding navigation and making it the perfect accompaniment on an adventure. It also highlights tourist information and points of interest, including viewpoints and pubs.

OS Landranger 1:50 000 (2cm to 1km or 1¼ inches to the mile)

OS Landranger aids the planning of the perfect short break in Great Britain and is a vital resource for identifying opportunities in both towns and countryside. It displays larger areas of the country than OS Explorer, making it more suitable for touring an area by car or by bicycle, helping you access the best an area has to offer.

OS Road 1:250 000 (1cm to 2.5km or 1 inch to 4 miles)

Ideal for navigating and planning any road journey, the OS Road series helps you get to your destination. The range covers the whole of Great Britain and shows all motorways, primary routes and A-roads, plus detailed tourist information including national parks, World Heritage Sites and a useful town and city gazetteer.

OS SHEET INDEX

	Puzzle map and feature	County/Council area	OS map sheet			Centre point	1 km reference
1	Happisburgh	Norfolk	252	133	5	TG 38304 31141	TG 38 31
2	Gough's Cave, Cheddar Gorge	Somerset	141	182	7	ST 46702 53923	ST 46 53
3	Preseli Hills	Pembrokeshire	OL35	145	6	SN 08244 34156	SN 08 32
4	Pegwell Bay	Kent	150	179	8	TR 33666 63169	TR 33 63
5	Norwich Castle	Norfolk	OL40	134	5	TG 23184 08524	TG 23 08
6	Bennachie	Aberdeenshire	421	38	1	NJ 66299 22654	NJ 66 22
7	Hadrian's Wall, Burgh by Sands	Cumbria	315	85	4	NY 31437 59223	NY 31 59
8	Offa's Dyke	Powys	201	148	6	SO 27304 62077	SO 27 62
9	York	York	290	105	4	SE 60471 51476	SE 60 51
10	Battle	East Sussex	124	199	8	TQ 74916 15520	TQ 74 15
11	Oxford	Oxfordshire	180	164	5	SP 51523 06369	SP 51 06
12	Runnymede	Surrey	160	176	8	TQ 00546 72243	TQ 00 72
13	Elderslie	Renfrewshire	342	64	3	NS 44377 62934	NS 44 62
14	Weymouth	Dorset	OL15	194	7	SY 67742 79718	SY 67 79
15	London – Westminster	City of Westminster	173	176	8	TQ 29684 79175	TQ 29 79
16	Linlithgow	West Lothian	349	65	3	NT 00216 77350	NT 00 77
17	Stratford-upon-Avon	Warwickshire	205	151	6	SP 20136 55045	SP 20 55
18	Plymouth	City of Plymouth	108	201	7	SX 45190 55739	SX 45 55
19	Worcester	Worcestershire	204	150	6	SO 85070 54804	SO 85 54
20	London - Pudding Lane	City of London	173	176	8	TQ 32940 80777	TQ 85 54
21	Berkeley	Gloucestershire	167	162	6	ST 68478 99152	ST 68 99
22	London – Mayfair	City of Westminster	173	176	8	TQ 28383 80796	TQ 28 80
23	Steventon	Hampshire	144	185	8	SU 55106 47227	SU 55 47
24	Kirkcaldy	Fife	367	59	3	NT 27795 91735	NT 27 91
25	Shrewsbury	Shropshire	241	126	6	SJ 48293 13009	SJ 48 13
26	Loughborough	Leicestershire	246	129	5	SK 53323 19383	SK 53 19
27	Shildon	County Durham	305	93	4	NZ 23955 25512	NZ 23 25
28	Farne Islands	Northumberland	340	75	3	NU 24593 38968	NU 24 38
29	Newcastle upon Tyne	Newcastle upon Tyne	316	88	4	NZ 25075 64798	NZ 25 64
30	Kennington	Lambeth, London	161	176	8	TQ 30968 77763	TQ 30 77
31	Moss Side	Manchester	277	109	4	SJ 84068 95401	S J84 95
32	Tredegar	Blaenau Gwent	13	161	6	SO 14179 09265	SO 14 09
33	Scarborough	North Yorkshire	301	101	4	TA 04339 88260	TA 04 88
34	Jarrow	South Tyneside	316	88	4	NZ 33810 65438	NZ 33 65
35	Waterfoot	East Renfrewshire	334	64	3	NS 56167 54461	NS 56 54
36	Tyneham	Dorset	15	194	7	SY 88181 80338	SY 88 80
37	Liverpool	Liverpool	275	108	4	SJ 34462 90429	SJ 59 68
38	Watford Gap	Northamptonshire	222,223	152	5	SP 59954 68025	SP 59 68
39	Wembley	Brent, London	173	176	8	TQ 19376 85523	TQ 19 85
40	Glyder Fawr, Snowdonia	Gwynedd	OL17	115	6	SH 64235 57929	SH 64 57

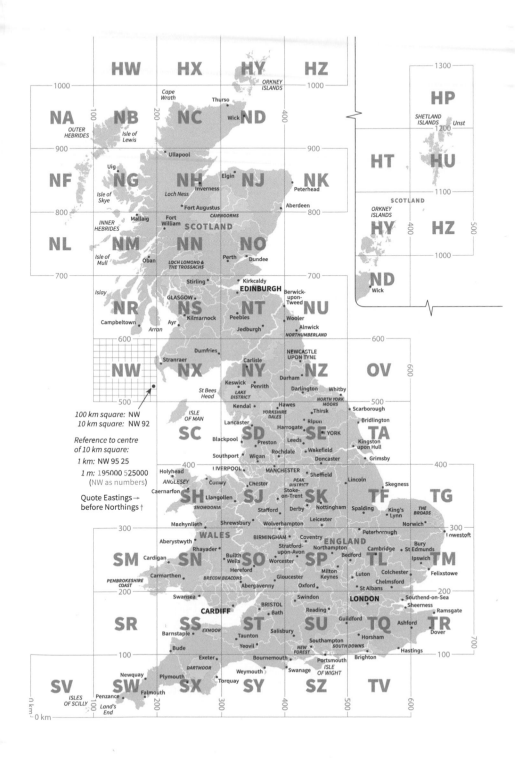

HW HX HY HZ
ORKNEY ISLANDS
1300
HP
SHETLAND ISLANDS Unst
1200

1000

NA NB NC ND
OUTER HEBRIDES
Isle of Lewis
Cape Wrath
Thurso
Wick

900

NF NG NH NJ NK
Ullapool
Uig
Isle of Skye
Loch Ness
Elgin
Inverness
Fort Augustus
Peterhead
Aberdeen

HT HU
SCOTLAND
ORKNEY ISLANDS

800

NL NM NN NO
INNER HEBRIDES
Isle of Mull
Mallaig
Fort William
CAIRNGORMS
SCOTLAND
Oban
LOCH LOMOND & THE TROSSACHS
Perth
Dundee

HY HZ
ND
Wick

700

NR NS NT NU
Islay
Campbeltown
Arran
Ayr
GLASGOW
Kilmarnock
Stirling
Kirkcaldy
EDINBURGH
Peebles
Jedburgh
Berwick-upon-Tweed
Wooler
Alnwick
NORTHUMBERLAND

600

100 km square: NW
10 km square: NW 92

Reference to centre of 10 km square:
1 km: NW 95 25
1 m: 195000 525000
(NW as numbers)

Quote Eastings→
before Northings ↑

NW NX NY NZ OV
Stranraer
Dumfries
Carlisle
NEWCASTLE UPON TYNE
St Bees Head
Keswick Penrith
LAKE DISTRICT
Durham
Darlington Whitby
NORTH YORK MOORS
Kendal
Hawes
YORKSHIRE DALES
Thirsk
Scarborough
Ripon
Bridlington

500

SC SD SE TA
ISLE OF MAN
Lancaster
Blackpool
Preston
Leeds
YORK
Harrogate
Southport
Wigan
Rochdale
Wakefield
Doncaster
Kingston upon Hull
Grimsby

400

Holyhead
ANGLESEY
Conwy
Chester
Sheffield
Lincoln
Skegness
Caernarfon
LIVERPOOL
MANCHESTER
PEAK DISTRICT
Stoke-on-Trent

SH SJ SK TF TG
SNOWDONIA
Llangollen
Stafford
Derby
Nottingham
Spalding
King's Lynn
THE BROADS
Machynlleth
Shrewsbury
Wolverhampton
Leicester
Norwich
Lowestoft

300

WALES
Aberystwyth
BIRMINGHAM
Coventry
Peterborough
ENGLAND
Rhayader
Stratford-upon-Avon
Northampton
Cambridge
Bury St Edmunds
Ipswich

SM SN SO SP TL TM
Cardigan
Builth Wells
Worcester
Bedford
Milton Keynes
Luton
Colchester
Felixstowe
Carmarthen
BRECON BEACONS
Hereford
Gloucester
Chelmsford
PEMBROKESHIRE COAST
Abergavenny
Oxford
St Albans

200

Swansea
CARDIFF
BRISTOL
Bath
Swindon
Reading
LONDON
Southend-on-Sea
Sheerness
Ramsgate

SR SS ST SU TQ TR
Barnstaple
EXMOOR
Taunton
Salisbury
Guildford
Ashford
Dover
Bude
Yeovil
Southampton
SOUTH DOWNS
Horsham
Hastings
NEW FOREST
Brighton

100

SV SW SX SY SZ TV
ISLES OF SCILLY
Penzance
Land's End
Falmouth
Newquay
Plymouth
Exeter
DARTMOOR
Torquay
Weymouth
Bournemouth
Swanage
Portsmouth
ISLE OF WIGHT

0 km

CREDITS

Trapeze would like to thank everyone at Orion who worked on the publication of *The Ordnance Survey Journey Through Time* in the UK.
Editorial: Jamie Coleman, Ru Merritt, Shyam Kumar, Sarah Fortune, Jane Hughes.
Copy editor: Ian Greensill. Proofreader: Abi Waters. Contracts: Anne Goddard.
Design: Helen Ewing, Julyan Bayes, Steve Marking, Nick May. Finance: Nick Gibson, Jasdip Nandra, Elizabeth Beaumont, Rabale Mustafa, Afeera Ahmed.
Marketing: Folayemi Adebayo. Production: Claire Keep, Fiona McIntosh. Publicity: Alainna Hadjigeorgiou. Sales: Jen Wilson, Esther Waters, Victoria Laws, Rachael Hum, Anna Egelstaff, Dominic Smith, Barbara Ronan, Maggy Park. Rights: Susan Howe, Krystyna Kujawinksa, Jessica Purdue.
Operations: Jo Jacobs, Sharon Willis.

ACKNOWLEDGEMENTS

Thank you to the many people who have worked
hard to make this book happen, including:

Nick Giles, Luretta Sharkey, Paul McGonigal, Mark Wolstenholme, Carolyne
Lawton, Daphne Berghorst, Grant Blakeley, Charlotte Brawn, Mandy Brereton,
Saskia Gooding, Richard Harper, Holly Price, Sam Lovell, Emily Bennett, Daisy
Smeddle, Sam Perkins, Bethany McAtee, David Jones and Camilla Dowson.

A huge thanks also to Adam Gauntlett.

Ordnance Survey

Fancy brushing up on your navigational skills and solving even more fiendish puzzles?

Why not get yourself copies of *The Ordnance Survey Puzzle Book, The Ordnance Survey Puzzle Tour of Britain* and *The Ordnance Survey Great British Treasure Hunt*, and pit your wits against Britain's greatest map makers?

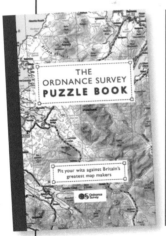

Share your adventures and puzzle-solving with us:

 os.uk/blog   @ordnancesurvey

@OSLeisure   @osmapping